Charles de Gaulle

Charles de Gaulle

Julian Jackson

HAUS PUBLISHING · LONDON

First published in Great Britain in 2003 by
Haus Publishing Limited
32 Store Street
London WC1E 7BS

The authors asserts his moral right to be identified as the author of this work

A CIP catalogue record of this work is available from the British Library

ISBN 1-904341-44-6

Typeset by Lobster Design

Printed and bound by Graphicom in Vicenza, Italy

Cover image: courtesy of Gamma/API Lochon
Back cover: courtesy of Ann Ronan Picture Library
Page iii: courtesy of Topham Picturepoint

Contents

Disobedience: 1890–1944

EARLY YEARS: 1890–1940

Charles de Gaulle enters History on 18 June 1940. Six weeks earlier, on 10 May, Germany had attacked France and rapidly overwhelmed the French forces. The French prime-minister, Paul Reynaud, wanted to take his government abroad and continue fighting alongside the British, rather than accept defeat. Failing to persuade his ministers to adopt this course of action, he resigned on 16 June. His successor, Marshal Philippe Pétain, immediately set about seeking the terms of an armistice with Germany. De Gaulle, who had been a member of Reynaud's cabinet, refused to accept that the war was over for France. On 17 June he left for London. At 6 pm on the following day, in studio 4B on the fourth floor of the BBC headquarters, he recorded his first appeal to the people of France. Four hours later it went out on air.

Although few people heard the speech, it is the founding moment of de Gaulle's career and of what came to be called 'Gaullism'. It opened: *The leaders who, for many years past, have been at the head of the French armed forces, have set up a government. Alleging the defeat of our armies, this government has entered into negotiations with the enemy with a view to bringing about a cessation of hostilities.* After going on to demonstrate why defeat was not inevitable, de Gaulle concluded: *I, General de Gaulle, now in London, call on all French officers and men who are at present on British soil, or may be in the future, with or without their arms; I call on all engineers and skilled workmen from the armaments factories who are present on British soil, or may be in the future, to get in touch with me. Whatever happens, the flame of French resistance must not and shall not die.*

Jeanne Maillot (1860–1940)
De Gaulle's mother

De Gaulle's broadcast was an extraordinary act of defiance against France's legally constituted government. Marshal Pétain was France's most venerated military leader; de Gaulle, almost unknown to the French public, was France's most junior general. De Gaulle later wrote of this moment: *as the irrevocable words flew out upon their way, I felt within myself a whole life come to an end. At the age of 49 I was entering an adventure like a man thrown by fate outside all frames of reference.*

But no one, however extraordinary, is entirely 'outside all frames of reference'. De Gaulle can be placed in a context – of family, generation and geography. He was

The Revolution of 1789 bequeathed to France a legacy of chronic political instability. Having abolished the absolute monarchy of the Bourbons, the revolutionaries experimented with a constitutional monarchy, a republic and an empire. This cycle was repeated during the 19th century with the Bourbon restoration of 1815–30, the July Monarchy of 1830–48, the Second Republic of 1848–52, and the Second Empire of 1852–70. The fall of the Second Empire after defeat by Prussia in 1870 led to the setting up of the Third Republic. Although the

Third Republic proved to have greater durability than any other regime since 1789, it was periodically rocked by political crises (the 'Boulanger Affair' in the mid-1880s, the 'Dreyfus Affair' from 1898 to 1902) in which the many people who remained nostalgic for monarchy or Empire tried to take their revenge.

These constitutional issues were bound up with the religious question. Since the Catholic Church had consistently opposed the Republic, the republicans were strongly anticlerical.

born in Lille on 22 November 1890. On his father's side he came from a minor aristocratic family – an ancestor had fought at Agincourt – which had lived in Paris since the 18th century. Its members had pursued careers as writers, scholars and civil servants. De Gaulle's paternal grandmother had been a prolific historian and novelist. On his mother's side de Gaulle was linked to the pious industrial bourgeoisie of Calais.

Henri de Gaulle (1848–1932)
De Gaulle's father

In 1890 France was an anti-clerical Republic, but de Gaulle was raised in an atmosphere of religion, learning and patriotism. His parents were monarchist and Catholic. His father taught in a Jesuit school; the young de Gaulle was partly educated there. Such circles abhorred the Republic and the Revolution from which it stemmed; the 'Marseillaise', the French national anthem originally composed for the Revolutionary army, was not approved in the de Gaulle household. De Gaulle would later write that he had been much afflicted by France's political divisions during his childhood. He directly experienced these when, in 1905, many Catholic schools were forced to close and he had to complete his education in Belgium. Of his parents, de Gaulle wrote: *My father was a thoughtful, cultivated, traditional man, imbued with a feeling of the dignity of France. He made me aware of her history. My mother had an uncompromising passion for her country, equal to her religious piety.* De Gaulle inherited, as a *second nature*, an *anxious pride* in France.

The Zeitgeist reinforced these family influences. During the

1900s there was a growing mood of nationalism in France as a result of the colonial rivalries between France and Germany in North Africa. A famous 1913 survey of the attitudes of French youth revealed the dominance of militaristic and patriotic values. This was an ardently patriotic, neo-romantic generation in revolt against 19th-century materialism and positivism. It read Nietzsche and the French nationalist writer Maurice Barrès; it thrilled to the heroic verse of Edmond Rostand, whose *Cyrano de Bergerac* de Gaulle knew by heart. Characteristic of the mood was Ernest Psichari, in whose novel *Appeal to Arms* (1913) the life of the soldier is invested with the solemnity of a religious vocation; during the 'phoney war' in 1939–40, waiting for the German offensive to begin, de Gaulle had a copy of Psichari's book sent to him. The most fashionable philosopher of the age was Henri Bergson, who attacked scientific materialism and celebrated 'intuition': visiting de Gaulle in 1969 the novelist André Malraux spotted the works of Bergson on his shelves.

Charles de Gaulle at St Cyr, 1910

Against this background a career in the army was a natural choice for de Gaulle. Through the army one could serve France without becoming excessively implicated in the Republic: regimes passed, the army endured. Having passed out of the St Cyr Military Academy, de Gaulle, whose grades would have allowed him to serve in the prized colonial army, chose instead a regiment based at Arras in northern France. The decision is revealing. Although de Gaulle was brought up in Paris, his family roots were in the north, and his notorious aloofness was partly a northern reserve. He frequently returned to the Lille/Calais area for holidays as a boy. When he married, in 1921, it was to Yvonne Vendroux, from a bourgeois Calais family very similar to his mother's. When he bought a house, in 1934, it was on the windy northeastern plains of Lorraine, in the village of Colombey-les-deux-Églises from where, as he wrote in his *War Memoirs,* he could contemplate the *vast, mournful horizons, melancholy woods and meadows.* De Gaulle was not one of those who celebrated *'la douce France'* ('the gentle land of France'). He preferred to dwell on the harshness and grandeur in France's geography. He had a predilection for bleak northern landscapes: so many of those garrulous Republican politicians he despised came from the sociable culture of the South.

Legends often gather around the early years of the famous. Of the young de Gaulle we know for certain that he stood out from his fellows by his height, by an awesome memory, and by an air of cold reserve. His brother Xavier commented that Charles must have been dropped in an icebox at birth. When a prisoner of war in his early twenties no one addressed him by the familiar 'tu' form; in 1924 one of his superiors commented: 'he spoils his undoubted talents by his excessive assurance, his contempt for other people's point of view, and his attitude of a king in exile'.[1] In his memoirs de Gaulle claims that he had a sense of destiny since adolescence – a conviction *that the interest in life consisted in one day rendering France some signal service and that I would have the occasion to do so.* This is not just an old man reinventing a young one: a text written by de Gaulle in 1905 describes how in 1930 'General de Gaulle', French Commander-in-Chief, vanquishes the German armies and avenges the defeat of France by Prussia in 1870. An early poem (1908) pleads: *when I die / Let it be on a field of battle.*[2]

When war came in 1914 de Gaulle, like so many of his generation, welcomed it. The outbreak of war caused a surge of national unity in France, a so-called 'sacred union'. *I admit,* de Gaulle wrote, *that in my first youth I pictured this unknown adventure with no horror, and magnified it in anticipation.* In reality war brought him more frustration than glory. In action he displayed the extraordinary indifference to physical danger which characterized his whole life. But after being wounded three times, he was taken prisoner in 1916. Five escape attempts failed because of his conspicuous height. In his 30 months of captivity de Gaulle read widely and lectured his fellow inmates (who included the future Soviet Marshal Tukachevsky) on military history. His joy at victory was mingled, as he told his mother, by *an indescribable regret . . .* [which] *will remain with me for the rest of my life* at not having played a larger part in it.[3] Perhaps because he had been spared some of the worst fighting of the Western Front, de Gaulle's memory of the War contained fewer of its horrors than that of his contemporaries: a certain pre-1914 innocence remained.

Charles de Gaulle: the youngest captain in the French army during World War One

De Gaulle's career between 1919 and 1940 is easily summarized: between 1919 and 1921 he served in the French military mission to Poland; in 1922 he lectured at St Cyr; between 1922 and 1924 he attended the Supreme War College, which trained the army's top officers; between 1925 and 1927 he served on Marshal Pétain's staff; in 1927 he was appointed commander of a light infantry battalion in Trier, western Germany; from 1929 to 1931 he was in the Levant (his only colonial posting); from 1932 he was on the Secretariat of the Supreme War Council for National Defence; in 1937, having been promoted colonel, he obtained command of a tank regiment at Metz in northeastern France.

What this steady, unspectacular ascent does not reveal is that de Gaulle had become in army circles quite a controversial figure. Soldiers were expected to be seen and not heard, but de Gaulle published four books in the inter-war years. The first, *The Enemy's House Divided* (*La Discorde chez l'ennemi*, 1924), is a piece of instant history – an examination of why Germany lost the war. *The Edge of the Sword* (*Le Fil de l'épée*, 1932), originating as a series of lectures at St Cyr, is a philosophical meditation on the nature of leadership. One key notion of this book – indeed its opening statement – is that in war, as in politics or economics, contingency is all. The essence of life is movement: no predetermined doctrine can respond effectively to what happens. Misunderstanding this, according to *The Enemy's House Divided,* had been one mistake of the German High Command in 1914. It follows from the unpredictability of events that leadership must contain a strong dose of intuition. The intellect in itself is insufficient since *the swift-moving and muddied torrent of circumstances can no more be imprisoned in its mesh than water in a fishing net.*[4] Leadership, in a view that shows the influence of Henri Bergson, is a kind of creative instinct.

The importance of flexibility is also a theme of de Gaulle's third book, *Towards an Army of the Future* (*Vers une armée de métier*, 1934). This book launched a sort of crusade against the defensive doctrine of the French High Command and advocated a professional army which used tanks as an offensive striking force – a French version of Blitzkrieg. This was the 'army of the future'. As military theory, these ideas were not as prescient as de Gaulle's admirers subsequently claimed – he did not, for example, foresee the importance of airpower in modern warfare – but he placed his arguments in a diplomatic and political context which took them beyond purely technical military issues. He argued that France's foreign policy, which was built around alliances with various East European states, required the possibility of taking offensive action to protect them; the alternative was appeasement of Germany. France needed a defence policy consistent with her diplomacy.

Even more shocking than the ideas he expressed was that, in attempting to promote them, de Gaulle directly lobbied leading politicians of all affiliations – Socialists, Christian Democrats and Conservatives. Although the only significant figure to take up his cause was the maverick conservative Paul Reynaud, it is revealing that de Gaulle was as ready to seek allies on the left as on the right.

To what extent did this mean that de Gaulle had moved away from the values of his upbringing? French politics had become deeply polarized in the 1930s, a period of political instability and social crisis. Right-wing anti-parliamentary organizations known as 'Leagues' demonstrated against Republican democracy and the Communists grew stronger in reaction against them. What little we know about de Gaulle's political views from his letters suggests that while he had little faith in the Republic as it was functioning, he was not tempted by the Leagues either. He was concerned at France's political divisions and saw that Fascism had been successful abroad in creating unity: but, as he wrote in 1937, *how can one accept that social order is purchased by the loss of liberty?*[5]

To understand de Gaulle's position on these matters, it is necessary to explore the roots of his nationalism in more detail. In the 1900s the two most prominent nationalist writers were the anti-

Republican polemicist Charles Maurras (1868–1952), founder of the movement Action Française, and the novelist Maurice Barrès (1862–1923). Both were obsessed with what they saw as the decadence of France and wanted revenge against Germany. But there were also important differences between them. Maurras was a pure counter-revolutionary: he advocated a restoration of the monarchy and believed that the rot had started with the French Revolution. Barrès, who started on the left, believed that it was impossible to turn the clock back in this way. His nationalism celebrated the cult of the 'soil and the dead'. Maurras's newspaper *Action Française* was the staple reading of the milieu in which de Gaulle was raised and he was attracted by Maurras's insistence on the need for a strong state, but otherwise he seems to have felt a greater affinity for the more ecumenical nationalism of Barrès, even indeed for the still more all-embracing nationalism of another key writer of the 1900s, Charles Péguy.

This emerges very clearly from de Gaulle's fourth book, *France and her Army* (*La France et son armée*), published in 1938. In this study of French history since the Gauls, seen through the history of her army, de Gaulle views the French past as a unity, and judges regimes dispassionately according to whether they contributed to the greatness of the nation: he generally views the *ancien régime*, especially of the 17th century, positively; admires the patriotism of the Revolutionary armies; sees the period 1815 to 1870 as a mediocre interlude between disasters; and praises the Third Republic up to 1918 for restoring French military strength, even as he deplores its political conflicts. Such views were not self-evident for someone from de Gaulle's background: the book's eulogy of the Revolutionary general Hoche attracted a sad rebuke from his father. The medieval historian Marc Bloch once remarked that there were 'two kinds of Frenchman who will never understand the history of France: those who refuse to thrill to the memory of the coronation [of the French Kings] at Reims; those who read the

Charles Péguy (1873-1914) was one of the intellectuals who threw themselves into the cause of defending Alfred Dreyfus, the Jewish French army captain wrongly accused of treason in 1894. He saw the struggle to prove Dreyfus's innocence as a spiritual crusade to preserve the purity of the Republican tradition. By 1904, however, he had come to deplore the way in which careerist politicians had appropriated Dreyfus's cause. As he put it: 'all begins in *mystique* and ends in *politique*'. In 1905, in the shadow of Franco-German rivalry, Péguy's book *Notre Patrie* (our country) celebrated patriotism, and distanced him from the internationalism of the Socialists with whom he had fought for Dreyfus. In 1910, he wrote a long poem about Joan of Arc that announced his conversion to Catholicism. But even as he moved towards a nationalist position, Péguy did not repudiate his earlier left-wing beliefs. Nationalist writers such as Barrès and Maurras were anti-Semitic and anti-Republican. But Péguy believed that all the traditions he had celebrated – Socialist, Jewish, Republican, Catholic – were part of the heritage of France. De Gaulle often quoted Péguy, and late in life he confided that *no writer has marked me as much . . . during my adolescence and when I was a cadet at St Cyr I read everything he wrote . . . I felt very close to him . . . He felt things exactly as I did.*

account of the *Fête de la Fédération* [The Festival of Federation, held during the Revolution] without feeling emotion'. De Gaulle was never one of those.

Given de Gaulle's instinctive nationalism, it is not surprising that he parted company from those many conservatives who increasingly saw appeasement of Hitler as a means of opposing Communism. De Gaulle never let anti-Communism blind him to the threat from Germany. He supported the Franco-Soviet Pact of 1936 and saw the agreement between Hitler and the British and French prime ministers at Munich in 1938 as a *terrible collapse of French power* that would only delay war.[6] When war did break out in September 1939 de Gaulle continued to be critical of what he considered the passivity of the French High Command. In January 1940 he addressed a memorandum to 80 leading politicians and officers drawing the lessons of the German blitzkrieg in Poland and reiterating his arguments for mobility in warfare. After the Germans attacked France in May, de Gaulle was given the command of a hastily formed tank division. The two battles fought by de Gaulle's armoured division were among the more distinguished moments in the lamentable performance of the French army. On 5 June, five days after being promoted to the rank of Brigadier-General, de Gaulle was appointed Under-Secretary of State for National Defence – his first

Promotion to Brigadier-General 1940

ever political appointment – in the government of Paul Reynaud. Despite his junior position, de Gaulle immediately impressed

On 13 May 1940 the German Panzers broke through the French defences on the River Meuse and forged across northeastern France towards the Channel. Two days later Colonel (as he still was) de Gaulle, in command of the Fourth Armoured Division, was ordered to launch a counterattack. De Gaulle was told: 'For you who have so long held the idea which the enemy is putting into practice, here is the chance to act'. On 17 May de Gaulle attacked the German columns near Montcornet, north of the river Aisne. The attack caught the Germans off guard, but they were able to fend it off easily enough, and it fizzled out after

24 hours. The same pattern occurred in two other attacks mounted by de Gaulle, one at Laon on 19 May and another at Abbeville on 28 May. Gaullist hagiographers who subsequently claimed that de Gaulle had nearly halted Rommel's tanks in their tracks are far wide of the mark. On the other hand, given that the Fourth Armoured Division had been hastily cobbled together only days earlier, consisted of units who had never trained together before, and lacked radios, anti-tank guns and air support, it was no discredit to de Gaulle that he had not been able to achieve more.

himself on the British as one of the most ardent opponents of the idea of signing an armistice with Germany. When Reynaud was replaced on 16 June by the pro-armistice Pétain, de Gaulle left for London – *alone . . . and stripped of everything, like a man on the beach proposing to swim across the ocean.*

RESISTANCE 1940–1942

The theme of de Gaulle's first broadcast from London was summed up in his later slogan: *France has lost a battle, she has not lost the war.* He argued that the conflict would become a world war since the British were not beaten and had the resources of the American economy at their disposal – and France still had her empire. De Gaulle urged those Frenchmen who wanted to go on

De Gaulle broadcasting to his countrymen from a BBC studio, 30 October 1941

De Gaulle's opposition to Pétain in 1940 had a long pre-history. The two men had known each other since before 1914. De Gaulle had served under Pétain in the 33rd Infantry Regiment at Arras in 1912. Pétain had a high regard for de Gaulle and after the war became his most powerful patron. The claim that Pétain was the godfather of his elder son, Philippe (born 1922), is incorrect, but de Gaulle certainly admired Pétain at this time. In 1922 Pétain commissioned him to ghostwrite a book on the history of the French army. To de Gaulle's annoyance, Pétain brought in other officers to contribute to the work and in 1928 he wrote Pétain a letter of extraordinary presumption, given the respective status of the two men, declaring that he was ready to see the book published under Pétain's name, with his contribution acknowledged, but he was not willing to work with anyone else. Since Pétain let the matter drop, de Gaulle decided in 1938 to publish the book under his own name as *France and her Army* – to Pétain's considerable irritation. The two men disagreed over the content of the book in revealing ways. At one point de Gaulle had written of the Revolution that it had deprived some generals of *prestige, often of life, sometimes of honour*. Pétain suggested moving 'life' to the end of the sentence. De Gaulle commented in the margin: *it is an ascending gradation: prestige, life, honour* (underlined three times). Their respective positions between 1940 and 1944 are encapsulated in this exchange.

fighting to join him in London. The broadcast had little effect, and five days later Pétain accepted an armistice with Germany. This divided France into an occupied and unoccupied zone. Within the 'free' zone the government moved to Vichy and the Republic committed suicide when parliament voted dictatorial powers to Pétain.

On 28 June Churchill recognized de Gaulle as leader of the 'Free French'. But, unlike other representatives of defeated nations in London, de Gaulle did not have the status of head of government in exile. Pétain remained France's legal head of government and the Foreign Office mistrusted Churchill's backing of de Gaulle in case it pushed Pétain closer to Germany. They were

Marshal Pétain, hero of the Great War and head of the Vichy government

not happy when de Gaulle's speeches began to attack Pétain with increasing ferocity.

For the Foreign Office de Gaulle was an unknown quantity. The Permanent Under-Secretary, Sir Alexander Cadogan, knew nothing about this obscure general except that 'he's got a head like a pineapple and hips like a woman'[7]; most French people, unable to see him, knew even less. Few people heard his 18 June speech; the BBC did not bother to record it. Given de Gaulle's total obscurity in 1940, Churchill's decision to back him was certainly quixotic. De Gaulle's personality appealed to Churchill's romantic imagination, and he had been genuinely impressed by his force of character on the few occasions they had met. But Churchill had also expected that de Gaulle would be joined by other more well-known French political figures. Only when they failed to materialize did he tell de Gaulle: 'you are alone, I shall recognize you alone'. Even many of those who did want to continue fighting had little confidence in this obscure dissident general: they preferred to go to North America. Jean Monnet, who had coordinated Anglo-French economic cooperation until the defeat, crossed the Atlantic, as did Alexis Léger, former head of the French Foreign Office. Among those who did rally to de Gaulle in 1940, there were no prefects or ambassadors, no academicians, no top civil servants or politicians. Nor did de Gaulle succeed in rallying the French empire: the governors of Syria, Indo-China and French North Africa stayed loyal to the government in Vichy. In September, de Gaulle launched an expedition with the British to win over the French port of Dakar in

West Africa. The failure of this operation, which showed that French troops loyal to Vichy would fire on their Free French compatriots, severely dented de Gaulle's prestige.

Despite these setbacks, de Gaulle was soon joined by individuals of varied but considerable talents. Gaullism, though also the adventure of an individual, was to assume the aspect of a brotherhood – a band of devoted followers or, as they came to be known, 'companions', many of whom would serve de Gaulle until his death. De Gaulle's first followers were strikingly diverse: they included Georges Boris, a left-wing economist who had been an adviser to the socialist Léon Blum; René Cassin, a 55-year-old jurist; Maurice Schumann, a left-wing Catholic journalist; Paul Reynaud's former adviser Gaston Palewski; Captain André Dewavrin, a 22-year-old lecturer from St Cyr; and Emile Muselier, a retired admiral. They were allocated tasks more or less suited to their expertise: Cassin became the Free French legal expert, Schumann a broadcaster, and Muselier head of the Free French naval forces. Dewavrin set up the Free French intelligence services. The leading personality to join de Gaulle was General

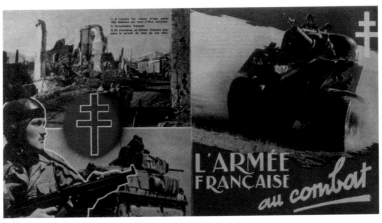

Free French poster in support of anti-Nazi war effort in France c. 1942–4. The poster contains the Free French cross of Lorraine symbol

Georges Catroux, a former colonial governor, whose negotiating talents softened the asperities of his new chief. He was an urbane figure who represented all that the British would have liked de Gaulle to be as they got to know him better.

One of de Gaulle's few early successes, in August 1940, was winning over French Equatorial Africa, which furnished him with a foothold outside England and a base from which Free French troops would eventually play a part in the North African campaigns. De Gaulle's aim, however, was never merely to play an auxiliary role in the Allied war effort. Cassin, enquiring about the legal status of the Free French, was told simply: *we are France.* This was not megalomania but a fundamental political statement, denying the legitimacy of the Vichy government and asserting de Gaulle's claim to be the provisional trustee of France's true interests. Possessing no significant military resources, de Gaulle was immediately pushed into a political role. His assessment of the future course of the war, whose outcome he could hardly influence, was remarkably accurate. From the outset he was thinking of the post-war situation and France's place in it: France must emerge as a first-rank power with her empire intact. The British did not always grasp this – as this dialogue with Churchill's adviser General Spears reveals: De Gaulle: *You think I am interested in England winning the war. I am not. I am only interested in French victory.* Spears: 'They are the same.' De Gaulle: *Not at all; not at all in my view.*[8] For de Gaulle an Allied victory was a necessary but not sufficient condition of French victory.

With French interests under attack from every side, de Gaulle believed he had only one weapon: total intransigence. When Churchill urged him to be more accommodating, he replied: *You can do it because you are seated on a solid state, an assembled nation, a united Empire . . . But me! Where are my resources? . . . I am too poor to be able to bow.* Or as Churchill later wrote: 'he had to be rude to the British to prove to French eyes that he was not a British puppet.' At the time Churchill was less able to take such a detached view and his relations with de Gaulle rapidly deteriorated: 'the cross of Lorraine [symbol of the Free French] was the heaviest cross I ever had to bear', he once remarked. Even those well-disposed to de Gaulle frequently found him intolerable: 'never seen anything like it in rudeness since Ribbentrop', said Anthony Eden on one occasion; 'stiff, rude and arrogant . . . a bloody man in his obstinacy, vanity and lack of diplomacy', commented another generally sympathetic British diplomat.[9] General Spears, who knew him well, wrote of de Gaulle at this time: 'He developed a dislike of

De Gaulle in London during the war

being liked as if it were a weakness, as if any acknowledgement of friendliness was to concede to someone a hold over him, so much so that there were times when he tried hard to foster dislike by indulging in deliberate rudeness.'[10] De Gaulle bit the hand that fed him because it was his only means of showing that France still had teeth.

Although there was a degree of calculation in all this – *with the English one must bang on the table and they will submit*, de Gaulle observed in 1941[11] – the vehemence of some of de Gaulle's reactions also had psychological causes. For someone of de Gaulle's temperament, his total dependence on the British was intolerably difficult to bear. One observer commented of him at this time: 'He felt the dishonour of his country as few men can feel anything, as Christ according to the Christian faith took on himself the sins of the world. I think he was like a man, during these days, who had been skinned alive and that the slightest contact with friendly well-meaning people got him on the raw to such an extent that he wanted to bite . . . The discomfort that I felt in his presence was due, I am certain, to the boiling misery and hatred inside him.'[12]

The first clash with Britain occurred in June 1941 during a joint British and Free French operation against Syria, where Pétain's government had allowed Germany to use French air bases. As at Dakar in 1940, the defending Vichyite forces resisted vigorously. After four weeks they surrendered and signed an armistice which hardly mentioned the Free French. De Gaulle, who saw this as *a pure and simple transference of Syria to the British*, reacted furiously, threatening to withdraw his troops from British command. Churchill wondered if he had 'gone off his head'. In fact de Gaulle's grievances were not completely unfounded. He was understandably resentful that the armistice had given him little opportunity to recruit from the defeated Vichyite forces who were repatriated to France.

De Gaulle succeeded in having the armistice revised, but the local British authorities were tardy at implementing it: in one place the British commander moved into the French residency, replacing the Tricolour with the Union Jack. De Gaulle sent a force to reclaim it, even at the risk of employing force against the British. Yet, despite an understandable sensitivity to possible Vichy accusations that he was betraying French imperial interests to Britain, de Gaulle was wrong to suspect some high-level British plot to supplant France in the Middle East. If the violence of his reactions did produce results, a more measured response might have achieved the same without also forfeiting British goodwill. As far as his future relationship with Churchill went, he had won a battle but nearly lost a war.

Churchill: You say you are France! You are not France! I did not recognize you as France.

De Gaulle: *Why are you discussing these questions with me if I am not France . . . I am acting in the name of France. I am fighting alongside England. I am not fighting for England.*

30 September 1942

The Middle East remained a running sore in relations between the British and de Gaulle. In June 1942 he even contemplated moving Free French headquarters to the Soviet Union, which had entered the war a year earlier. One French observer in London commented at this time: 'the General must be constantly reminded that our number one enemy is Germany. If he followed his natural inclination, it would rather be the British.'[13] In their disputes with de Gaulle, the British would periodically retaliate by preventing him from broadcasting, forbidding him to leave the country or depriving him of intelligence information. They played on rivalries among the Free French, especially those who resented de Gaulle's authoritarian style. Among these was the scheming Admiral Muselier, who played his cards badly and was excluded from the Free French in 1942. Churchill conceived the idea of 'putting the General in commission' – making de Gaulle set up a formal committee that would limit his power. This also backfired: although in September 1941 de Gaulle did set up a 'National Committee', he remained in control and now had the additional authority that came from presiding over an embryo government.

As his difficulties with Churchill developed in 1941, de Gaulle tried to court America.[14] In June he proposed that if Roosevelt did enter the war he might prefer French Equatorial Africa to Britain as a base of operations. But hopes of playing America off against Britain came to nothing. On the contrary, America's entry into the war in December 1941 compounded de Gaulle's difficulties with the Allies. Roosevelt was suspicious of the 'so-called Free French' (as his Secretary of State called them). He doubted de Gaulle's democratic credentials and his utility to the Allied cause: Dakar and Syria had demonstrated that Gaullist involvement in operations against Vichy-controlled areas could be counter-productive. American policy was to retain contacts with Vichy in the hope of bringing Pétain round to an anti-German position.

Tensions between de Gaulle and Roosevelt were aggravated by de Gaulle's decision, in December 1941, to send a force to recover the two tiny French-owned islands of Saint-Pierre-et-Miquelon, off the Newfoundland coast. Roosevelt opposed this action as liable to alienate Vichy. A compromise was reached, but it left simmering grievances on both sides.

When planning their invasion of French North Africa in November 1942, the Americans insisted on excluding de Gaulle. He was not even informed in advance. Instead, American officials cultivated the local Vichy authorities, gambling on their cooperation after the landings. In the event, American forces encountered bitter resistance which ended only when Pétain's representative, Admiral Darlan, who happened to be in Algeria, switched sides and ordered a ceasefire. In line with Roosevelt's policy of dealing with the devil if this would save lives, the Americans then installed Darlan as high commissioner in North Africa.

Darlan's appointment shocked Anglo-American public opinion, since he had been particularly pro-German in 1941. Roosevelt's description of him as merely a 'temporary expedient' did little to help, and [Darlan's assassination in December] resolved an embarrassing situation. De Gaulle certainly did not regret Darlan's death, but there is no evidence that he had a hand in it, as has often been accused. The Americans replaced Darlan with General Giraud, impeccably anti-German but politically naive: his main virtue was not being de Gaulle. This did little to appease public opinion. Roosevelt and Churchill, meeting near Casablanca in January 1943, therefore decided to bring the two generals together, and Churchill summoned de Gaulle from London. De Gaulle viewed Churchill's invitation as an intolerable interference in internal French affairs and initially refused to come, humiliating Churchill in Roosevelt's eyes. But de Gaulle retained a shrewd sense of how far intransigence could be pushed and finally he allowed himself to be persuaded to leave for North Africa. There,

Giraud, Roosevelt, de Gaulle and Churchill at Casablanca, January 1943. De Gaulle and Giraud were barely on speaking terms

for the first time, he met Roosevelt (unaware that during their interview armed American agents were concealed behind a curtain, so suspicious were the Americans of this general). De Gaulle agreed to sign a joint communiqué with Giraud and be photographed shaking his hand. The world's press was temporarily placated, but nothing had been solved: de Gaulle returned to London and Giraud remained in Algiers.

Roosevelt was amused by what he considered the antics of the two prima donna generals, the 'bride' and the 'groom' as he called them. He cabled Washington that 'temperamental Lady de Gaulle' had been 'quite snooty'. This was as unperceptive as it was patronizing: serious issues of principle were at stake. For Roosevelt, France as a state was out of the war and Giraud or de Gaulle were useful if they could rally forces previously loyal to

Vichy. The political future of France was an open question to be resolved after victory. For de Gaulle, however, unless the political existence of the French state were invoked at every stage, France would be defenceless against the whims of the Allies once the war was over. He was right to be worried. Roosevelt, besides having designs on the French empire, was also toying with the idea of creating a new state called Wallonia out of Belgium, Luxembourg and part of northeastern France. Such ideas, of which de Gaulle was blissfully unaware, might well have come to nothing, but without someone authorized to speak on behalf of the French state at the end of the war there would have been little the French could have done to resist them.

There was another issue at stake in the conflict between de Gaulle and Roosevelt. The Americans underestimated the revulsion in Europe at the phenomenon of collaboration and the hatred that the emerging Resistance felt towards morally tainted 'temporary expedients' like Darlan. Here de Gaulle the French conservative found himself giving lessons to Roosevelt the Wilsonian idealist. As he said during the Darlan affair: *You invoke strategic reasons, but it is a strategic error to place oneself in a situation contradictory to the moral character of the war. We are no longer in the 18th century when Frederick the Great paid the courtier of Vienna in order to be able to take Silesia, nor in the Italian Renaissance when one hired the myrmidons of Milan or the mercenaries of Florence. In any case we do not put them at the head of a liberated people. Today we make war with our blood and souls and the suffering of nations.*

This kind of language showed that de Gaulle's ideas had evolved since 1940. The rhetoric of his first London broadcasts had been patriotic not ideological: the key words were 'honour and fatherland' (the Free French motto). From October 1940 de Gaulle's position was that after the war the French the people should choose their own constitutional arrangements, but he did not use the word 'democracy' before September 1941 nor 'Republic' before April 1942. In 1940 de Gaulle still felt little attachment to a Republic which had presided over so humiliating a military collapse. When his follower René Cassin tried to obtain a more open commitment to democracy, he was told that the French people currently identified democracy with the fallen Republic which *has been condemned by the facts and public opinion.*[15] During 1942, however, de Gaulle's speeches became increasingly radical. He talked of *liberty, equality and fraternity* (November 1941), of France *betrayed by her leaders and privileged* (June 1942), of *the people against the Bastille* (June 1943). The word 'revolution' appears seven times in his speeches in April 1942 alone; at a press conference in February 1943 he referred favourably to the Republic twelve times.

Why did this change occur? 1941 had witnessed the growth of Resistance movements in France, and their spirit was deeply anti-conservative, especially after June 1941 (date of Hitler's invasion of Russia) when the French Communist Party (PCF) joined them.

Initially the Free French knew little of what was going on in France, and de Gaulle had not originally given much thought to the possibilities of clandestine activity in France. This situation changed with the arrival in London of the high-ranking civil servant Jean Moulin, who informed de Gaulle of the potential offered by the internal Resistance. During 1942 Resistance leaders paid visits to London to discover more about de Gaulle's political ideas. De Gaulle and the Resistance had much to gain from each other. For the Resistance, de Gaulle could provide both material support and a

French Resistance leader Jean Moulin who was tortured to death in 1945

mobilizing symbol to use against the myth of Pétain: by January 1943 three million people were estimated to listen to his broadcasts regularly. For de Gaulle, the support of the Resistance showed Roosevelt that he did genuinely speak for France. In January 1942 de Gaulle sent Moulin back to France as his representative to the Resistance. Moulin's mission was to unite the Resistance movements and bring them to support de Gaulle. To achieve this objective de Gaulle was ready to make certain accommodations. When the trade unionist resister Christian Pineau arrived in London in January 1942 he asked for a message to take back to France. De Gaulle's original draft was highly critical of the Third Republic, but at the last moment, just as Pineau was about to return to France, he agreed to modify his text and insert a reference to the *French ideal of liberty, equality and fraternity*. Just as Henry IV had concluded that Paris was worth a mass, so de Gaulle took the view that Algiers was worth a Republic. In 1943 he took this policy further by receiving in London Fernand Grenier of the PCF and writing a warm letter to the Party's Central Committee. Winning the support of the Communists now became an important part of de Gaulle's strategy.

De Gaulle's political radicalization was not only expedient. He genuinely resented what he saw as France's betrayal by her elites: *I did not see many of you in London, gentlemen* he told a delegation of business leaders after the war. Even if de Gaulle's political evolution was partly opportunistic, he understood the need to adapt while Giraud did not: in their joint communiqué Giraud had objected to the inclusion of the phrase 'democratic principles'. As de Gaulle wrote later of Giraud: *the elemental, revolutionary character of the internal resistance was incomprehensible to him.*

LIBERATION: 1943–1944

During 1943 de Gaulle's energies were absorbed by the struggle for power with Giraud. De Gaulle could rely on no support from

Churchill who, under Roosevelt's influence, was close to breaking with de Gaulle entirely. The Foreign Office, in a reversal of the 1940 situation, now backed de Gaulle and Foreign Secretary Anthony Eden became a useful ally. Nonetheless de Gaulle was forbidden to leave London until the end of May and so General Catroux went to negotiate with Giraud in Algiers. The support of the Resistance strengthened de Gaulle's hand. In May, shortly before his arrest by the Gestapo, Moulin had succeeded in bringing the many resistance movements together into a National Resistance Council (CNR) which also included representatives of French political parties. This body recognized de Gaulle as 'sole leader of French resistance' and demanded the installation of a provisional government under his presidency in Algiers.

There were two important issues between de Gaulle and Giraud. First, de Gaulle demanded a purge of the leading Vichy supporters from posts of authority in Algiers. Second, he insisted on establishing a single political entity to represent French interests, something which clashed with the American desire to deal with whatever local French authorities they found. Giraud, who simply wanted to bring French forces back into the war against Germany, did not object to the American line; for de Gaulle the political issue remained fundamental. The two men finally reached an agreement at the end of May. A French Committee of National Liberation (CFLN) was to be set up in Algiers under their joint presidency. Before leaving London, which had been his base for three years, de Gaulle had a final meeting with Eden which he describes in characteristic terms in his memoirs: *Mr Eden good-humouredly asked me: 'Did you know that you have caused us more difficulties than all our other European allies combined?' 'I don't doubt it,' I replied, smiling in my turn. 'France is a great power.'*

Once in Algeria de Gaulle gradually outmanoeuvred the hapless Giraud and gained full control over the CFLN. By the end of July de Gaulle had become sole president; in November Giraud lost his place on the Committee entirely. De Gaulle set about turning the CFLN into a government that could assume power in liberated France. He broadened its political base, going as far in March 1944 as to include two Communists. He also set up a

Consultative Assembly to act as a sort of provisional parliament. From July 1943 de Gaulle consistently referred to the CFLN as the government and to Vichy as the so-called government. Vichy's claims to be an independent government were indeed increasingly hollow. Since November 1942 the Germans had occupied the whole of France, and were conscripting huge numbers of French workers into German factories; the ranks of the Resistance swelled in consequence. De Gaulle, having absorbed the Vichyite French army in North Africa, now had some

General de Gaulle with members of the CFLN in Algeria in November 1943

400,000 troops at his disposal. In May 1944, the CFLN declared itself the Provisional Government of the French Republic (GPRF).

The main barrier to de Gaulle's hopes remained Roosevelt. Only with great difficulty could the latter be persuaded in August 1943 to grant the CFLN even limited recognition – far short of accepting its status as a provisional government. Roosevelt wanted liberated France to be treated as a defeated country, run by an American military administration (AMGOT). American officials were receiving crash courses in how to become French administrators, and a special occupation currency was prepared. De Gaulle meanwhile was preparing his own lists of 'Commissioners of the Republic' who would represent the GPRF in liberated France; he was incensed at the idea of the Americans issuing their own currency for France. Churchill oscillated between his loyalty to Roosevelt and the inclinations of his own government. His attitude to de Gaulle, though mercurial, was quite different from Roosevelt's icy suspicion.

Returning to Britain on the eve of the Normandy landings, de Gaulle had stormy meetings with Churchill and the Supreme Allied Commander Dwight Eisenhower, who, though personally sympathetic to de Gaulle, had to obey the instructions of his president. A furious row broke out over the wording of the proclamation Eisenhower intended to make on D-day, which made no reference to any French authority, and invited the French people to execute his orders. De Gaulle was also enraged that his own message was to be broadcast last, after those of Eisenhower and the heads of state of the other countries of occupied Europe. He riposted that he would broadcast at an entirely different time from everyone else, and would not allow Free French liaison officers to land with the Allied troops. Churchill was at one point ready to send de Gaulle back to Algiers 'in chains if necessary'. One Foreign Office official who was sympathetic to de Gaulle commented: 'we always start by putting ourselves in the wrong and then de Gaulle puts himself more in the wrong. He deserves to lose the rubber.'[16] When D-day, 6 June 1944, arrived no agreement had yet been reached on how France was to be administered.

In the end, de Gaulle broadcast to the French people on 6 June at 5.30 pm, eight hours after Eisenhower. Ordering them to obey the orders given by the 'French government', and making no mention of the American troops, he proclaimed: *the supreme battle*

General de Gaulle visits Normandy, June 1944

is engaged . . . it is France's battle and it is the battle for France . . . it is a battle that the French will fight with fury. He knew of course that there were no French troops among the forces landing in France on D-day.

Once the Allies had established a bridgehead in Normandy, de Gaulle was permitted on 14 June to pay a brief visit to Normandy. Churchill apologized to Montgomery for 'inflicting' de Gaulle on him for a day, and warned him to make no concessions. On the boat to France de Gaulle was silent. To break the ice, one aide observed that it was four years to the day that the Germans had arrived in Paris. *Well, they were wrong*, snapped de Gaulle in reply.[17]

During his day in Normandy, de Gaulle succeeded in establishing the authority of his representatives: AMGOT was stillborn. This was not a foregone conclusion. De Gaulle had been an unknown figure four years before and his appearance was not familiar yet. In the jeep taking him to Bayeux, he was accompanied by General Béthouart who, being

On 23 August 1944 de Gaulle was heading from Le Mans in the direction of Paris. Everywhere there were crowds to greet him. At one point a man rushed up to cheer him with the words 'Long live the Marshal' – that is, Pétain. De Gaulle turned to an aide and remarked: *One can hardly blame them for getting confused.*

senior in rank, had five stars on his kepi while de Gaulle only had two. A bystander approached, wrongly assuming Béthouart to be de Gaulle. To avoid any further embarrassment, de Gaulle hailed two bemused gendarmes, told them who he was and instructed them to announce his imminent arrival in Bayeux. They pedalled off to do so, and by the time of de Gaulle's arrival, a respectable enough crowd of cautious Normans had gathered. Most of them, having probably passed a less than heroic four years, were flattered, bemused – and possibly a bit alarmed – to hear de Gaulle tell them that they must go on fighting *as you have never ceased to do since the start of the war.*

De Gaulle described this first encounter with the French people in the following terms: *We went down the street on foot. At the sight of General de Gaulle, the inhabitants stood in a kind of daze, then burst into cheers or into tears. Coming out of their houses, they followed me in*

Crowds line the streets in support of de Gaulle on his return to Paris in August 1944

the grip of an extraordinary emotion. The children surrounded me. The women were smiling and sobbing. The men held out their hands. We moved on together, all overwhelmed by this sense of fraternity, as we felt the joy, the pride, the hope of the nation rise again from the depths of the abyss.

Allied military observers also reported de Gaulle's popularity, albeit in somewhat more sober terms. At Bayeux he installed his own Commissioner of the Republic in order to circumvent any American civil administration. At the local level Allied officers accepted this *fait accompli* and started to work with his representatives. Having backed him in 1940 when his enterprise was a dream, the Allies found they could not ditch him in 1944 once it had become a reality.

Government and Opposition: 1944–1958

HEAD OF THE PROVISIONAL GOVERNMENT: 1944–1946

I am the only revolutionary in France, de Gaulle told his young aide Claude Mauriac in October 1944. His political rhetoric certainly had radicalized since 1940, but his immediate preoccupation in liberated France was to restore the authority of the State: order not revolution. He wanted to send a firm message to any Communist resisters tempted to exploit the void left by the collapse of the Vichy regime, and by the same token to show the Allies that, far from being a Communist stooge, he was their most effective bulwark against Communism.

By mid-August, Allied forces were within reach of Paris. Eisenhower originally intended to skirt the city so as not to slow up his advance, but de Gaulle persuaded him to change this plan and allow Free French troops to lead the Allies into Paris. Paris was symbolically important, but de Gaulle also wished to pre-empt an insurrection by the Resistance which could have developed into a bloodbath or profited the Communists. Another fear was that Roosevelt, ever keen to circumvent de Gaulle, might recognize some rump government of Third Republic politicians in Paris before de Gaulle had arrived.

De Gaulle entered Paris on 25 August. At the Hôtel de Ville, seat of revolutions in the 19th century, the CNR, representing the Resistance, was waiting to greet him. But de Gaulle, ever attentive to the importance of symbols, went first to the Ministry of Defence. In his *War Memoirs* he commented implausibly that everything was as he had left it four years before: *not a piece of furniture, not a rug, not a curtain had been disturbed. Nothing was missing except the State. It was my duty to restore it: I installed my staff and got down to work.* He then proceeded to the Police headquarters and only finally to the Hôtel de Ville: first the site of State power, then the site of Resistance power. Asked to proclaim the restoration of the Republic from the balcony, he refused on the grounds *that the Republic has never ceased to exist.* His point was that if Vichy, as he argued, had never been legitimate, he had represented the continuity of France since 1940. To 'restore' the Republic would have been to accept that Vichy had existed.

On the next day, de Gaulle organized a procession down the Champs Elysées. Having demonstrated that the Resistance was subordinate to the state, de Gaulle now intended to show that his legitimacy derived not from it but directly from the people. Apart from some shots mysteriously fired during a service de Gaulle attended in Notre Dame, the day was a massive success: over a

De Gaulle's procession down the Champs Elysées, 26 August 1944

million people turned out to cheer him. De Gaulle ensured that Georges Bidault, President of the CNR, was a few steps behind him in the parade.

De Gaulle continued the process of taming the Resistance by taking some of its members into his provisional government and incorporating the Resistance fighters into the regular army. In the autumn, de Gaulle embarked on an extensive regional tour to bolster his government's authority, especially in the south where local liberation committees were reluctant to hand over power to

Cover of booklet issued by the French Ministry of War celebrating the liberation of Alsace and Lorraine 1944 and 1945

de Gaulle's commissioners. The truculence that de Gaulle had previously visited on the Allies as the incarnation of France, he now visited on regional Resistance leaders as incarnation of the State. In Marseilles, reviewing a local guerrilla army, he muttered, *What a farce*; in Toulouse a ragged guerrilla officer was chastised: *Can't you sew?* There was in all this a northerner's dislike of southern exuberance, a professional officer's distaste for this improvised people's army, and, in a characteristic Gaullist phrase, *calculated solemnity*: the State cannot smile. One resister commented when he met de Gaulle in 1944: 'I have already witnessed human ingratitude in my life, but never on this scale.'[18] Order was restored remarkably fast. The final stage in the process was the dissolution in October 1944 of the so-called 'patriotic militia', paramilitary groups dominated by the Communists. 'The insurrectionary period is over', the government proclaimed. Despite rumblings of discontent, the Communists submitted. In his *War Memoirs*, written during the Cold War, de Gaulle implied that he had thwarted a Communist takeover of power. In fact the Communists never had such an aim, and de Gaulle probably knew it.

The most pressing task facing de Gaulle's government was to reconstruct a debilitated economy. With a transport system in chaos and severe shortages of food and fuel, the prospect of hyper-inflation loomed large. Within his government, two contrasting economic policies were proposed. The left-wing politician, Pierre Mendès France, Minister for Economic Affairs, advocated an austere policy: an exchange of all banknotes for a new currency worth one quarter of the old and a massive tax on capital. These measures were designed to nip inflation in the bud, destroy the black market and punish war profiteers. René Pleven, the Finance Minister, argued that after four years of hardship, this was too tough a medicine for the French people to swallow. In April 1945 de Gaulle finally arbitrated in favour of Pleven, and Mendès France resigned. This decision has rightly been seen as contributing to an inflationary spiral which was to plague France in the 1950s and has been blamed on de Gaulle's lack of interest in economic issues: *never again will I allow anyone to talk about economics at me for three hours*, he commented. But Pleven's claim that Mendès France's policy would have put intolerable strains on the social fabric and alien-

At Bourg-Blanc, a woman is cropped for having collaborated with the Germans

ated the Communists had much plausibility. Although it was not like de Gaulle to opt for the soft option, as he said of this affair, *in economics as in politics or strategy, there is no absolute truth . . . only circumstances.*

Pragmatism also governed de Gaulle's policy towards the *épuration* – the purge of those suspected of collaboration. The Resistance was vociferous in demanding it, and de Gaulle accepted its necessity as well. About 10,000 summary executions had occurred during the Liberation, many of them during the course of the fighting itself, but de Gaulle insisted that the process be quickly brought under government control and undertaken with as much clemency as possible in order to heal the nation's wounds. *France needs all her sons*, he declared. Of 7037 death sentences pronounced by the courts, he commuted 6270 (including that of Pétain himself). There is no truth in the allegations of Vichy apologists that at the Liberation de Gaulle presided over, and encouraged, a terrible bloodbath.

Pierre Pucheu had been Minister of the Interior in the Vichy government in 1941. Like some other high-ranking Vichy officials, in 1943 he changed sides and went over to North Africa, having been led to believe by Giraud that he would be welcomed and be allowed to serve with the Free French. Instead he was arrested, tried in a somewhat summary fashion and executed as a collaborator on 22 March 1944. Vichy apologists saw this as proof of de Gaulle's vengeful and unforgiving nature. But de Gaulle himself was not very happy about the affair – *We have blood on our hands,* he remarked to one resister – and on other occasions he was more than ready to make use of people who had served Vichy (including his own future Foreign Minister Maurice Couve de Murville). The problem with Pucheu was the allegation that he had in 1941 selected French Communist hostages to be shot by the Germans in reprisal for Communist attacks on their troops. Understandably, the Communists, whose support de Gaulle needed at this stage, had a particular hatred for him. De Gaulle was not sanguinary, but he could be ruthlessly unsentimental if circumstances demanded.

De Gaulle's brusque treatment of the Resistance, his choice of *laissez-faire* economics over austerity, and his inclination for moderation in the purge led to accusations that having used the Resistance he then 'betrayed' it. But the Resistance was politically heterogeneous, and once the Germans had been driven out, its members shared little more than a mystique. Inasmuch as the Resistance possessed a concrete programme, it was expressed in the 1944 Charter of the CNR which demanded extensive nationalizations, a social security system and economic planning. During the 18 months of de Gaulle's provisional government much of this agenda was carried out. The Renault company, the Nord coal mines, air transport, the Bank of France and the four main private banks were nationalized, and nationalization of electricity and gas was prepared; a social security system was implemented; women were granted the vote; and, finally, in January 1946, de Gaulle accepted the proposal of the economist Jean Monnet to set up an economic planning commissariat.

This was one of the most radical periods of economic and social change in French history, quite as far-reaching as that being instigated by Britain's post-war Labour government. It may be that in the atmosphere of post-Liberation France, de Gaulle had little choice in the matter; that his government acted more cautiously than some resisters desired; and that, as he later said – when wishing to cast himself in a conservative light – he had implemented these measures to undercut the Communists. But it cannot be simultaneously alleged that he betrayed the Resistance; up to a point he gave reality to its aspirations.

Nonetheless it is true that de Gaulle's priorities in 1944 were different from those of the Resistance. The mood of the Resistance was perfectly encapsulated by the newspaper *Combat*, whose motto was 'from resistance to revolution'. Where it invoked 'human dignity', 'solidarity' and 'justice', de Gaulle invoked the authority of the State and the prestige and greatness of France. He had a revealing interchange with Claude Mauriac in October 1944. Mauriac had drafted a letter for de Gaulle's signature talking of 'France purified and returned to honour and liberty'. De Gaulle protested, *You speak of liberty, honour, purification . . . But what about victory? What I see above all is France victorious.*[19] Similarly he deplored the fact that Pétain's trial had concentrated on the repressive aspects of the Vichy regime rather than on the *capital error* of the armistice. As de Gaulle once observed: *Pétain stayed in France to look after the shop. But that wasn't what mattered. What mattered was France.* De Gaulle always put 'France' above the temporary discomforts of the French. The fact that the war continued for another eight months after the liberation of Paris was for him an opportunity to be grasped: *That the war was to continue was certainly tragic from the point of view of losses, damages and expenses which we French would still have to endure. But from the viewpoint of France's higher interests – which is something quite different from the immediate interests of the French – I did not regret it. For with the war dragging on, our aid would be necessary.* It is impossible to imagine Pétain uttering such words.

Inevitably the continuing war led to new friction with the Allies. Although by September 1944 most of France had been liberated, in December the Germans mounted a counteroffensive in the Ardennes. Eisenhower decided upon a tactical withdrawal which involved evacuation of the recently liberated city of Strasbourg. But Strasbourg, which had been German between 1871 and 1918, was as symbolically charged a city as Paris itself, and abandoning it would have been a terrible blow to morale. De Gaulle therefore refused: military considerations were secondary to politics. Thanks partly to Churchill's support (which he admits grudgingly in his memoirs) de Gaulle prevailed. Once the German counter-offensive collapsed, de Gaulle sought to ensure that French troops were in at the kill. General de Lattre de Tassigny was ordered to cross the Rhine even if *the Americans don't*

General de Gaulle greets Allied commanders in France including General Dwight Eisenhower. Despite the handshakes, relations were frosty

assist and you have to do it in barges. French troops eventually pen-etrated into southern Germany, leading to a new row with Eisenhower, who insisted they withdraw from Stuttgart which was assigned to the American zone.

De Gaulle's bitter-ness against the Allies in this period was immense. He told Mauriac in September 1944: *they are betraying us, they are betraying Europe, the bastards. But they shall pay me for it.*[20] He resented the Allies' slowness in for-mally recognizing the GPRF – which, owing to Roosevelt's reluc-tance, did not occur until October 1944 – and their unwillingness to provide the French army with all the arms it needed. Once his government had been officially recognized, de Gaulle was able to embark on a foreign policy, whose overriding aim was, of course, to restore France's 'rank'.

De Gaulle's experience during the war had convinced him that it would be difficult to drive a wedge between Britain and America. He frequently returned to a remark that Churchill had allegedly made to him on the eve of the Normandy landings: 'each time we must choose between Europe and the open sea, we shall always choose the open sea. Each time I must choose between you and Roosevelt, I shall choose Roosevelt.' De Gaulle instead turned to Russia. In December 1944 he visited Moscow, and returned to France having signed a Treaty of Friendship with Stalin. Although this was dramatic evidence of France's return to the world diplomatic stage, its practical consequences were minimal: de Gaulle had wanted Soviet backing for his ideas about a post-war settlement for Germany but Stalin refused to commit himself to anything without consulting America or Britain; as for 'friendship' towards France, Stalin demonstrated little of that during the 1945 conferences at Yalta and Potsdam. France was invited to neither gathering, to de Gaulle's fury. After Yalta he signalled his displeasure by refusing Roosevelt's invitation to meet him at Algiers where the president had stopped off on his return to America.

In fact the results of Yalta and Potsdam were remarkably favourable to France, despite Stalin and thanks entirely to British lobbying. The French obtained a zone in occupied Germany, and were granted permanent membership (with Britain, America, Russia and China) of the Security Council of the newly founded

1944 · LIBÉRATION · 1944

AUX FORCES FRANÇAISES DE L'INTÉRIEUR · LA NATION RECONNAISSANTE

Commemorative poster celebrating the liberation of France 1944

United Nations. But, although no definite solution to Germany's future had been agreed at the end of 1945, the Allies had not gone for de Gaulle's solution: that Germany should be broken up into autonomous states. The decisions taken at Yalta and Potsdam were a formal recognition of France's great-power position, even if her exclusion from the taking of these decisions was a practical recognition of her junior status (and her negligible role in Germany's defeat). This was probably more than would have been achieved without the existence of de Gaulle, but less than he desired. He wrote, *The British considered themselves as participants in a game to which we were not admitted.* Having got nowhere with Stalin, towards the end of 1945 he aired the idea of a sort of Western European bloc to play a balancing role between the superpowers. His overriding aim was to bring France back to the world stage.

Another possible source of French influence was its empire which de Gaulle had defended against all opponents – real and imaginary – since 1940. Once again this led to major conflict with Britain. When the Free French recovered Syria in 1941 they had promised independence to the Arabs. But de Gaulle first wanted to negotiate France a privileged military status in the area. As a result, in 1945 there were violent nationalist protests which French troops suppressed brutally: the British intervened to prevent further bloodshed and imposed a ceasefire. This episode inspires some of the angriest pages of de Gaulle's memoirs, castigating the *passionate ambition* of the British to be *sole masters of the East*. He told the British ambassador that unfortunately France was not in a position to wage war on Britain but that *you have outraged France and betrayed the West. That cannot be forgotten.* De Gaulle's interpretation of these events was tendentious: Arab nationalism was not a British creation and Churchill had intervened most reluctantly. It is true, however, that many pro-Arab British officials did want to oust the French from the area, and although Churchill harboured no strategy to destroy French influence in the Levant, he was concerned not to alienate Arab support. British policy was confused rather than malevolent but its political consequences were not so different from what de Gaulle feared.

In French Indo-China, France's position was equally fragile. After the Japanese surrender, Vietnamese nationalists under Ho Chi Minh had declared a provisional government, with the approval of the anti-colonialist Americans. In August 1945, de Gaulle despatched a French expeditionary force to restore French sovereignty and sent out Admiral Thierry d'Argenlieu to be high commissioner. De Gaulle's idea was to restore the former Emperor, deposed by the French in 1916, as a nominally independent monarch allied to France. This idea came to nothing, but after de Gaulle had left power in 1946, d'Argenlieu, with de Gaulle's tacit approval, schemed to block any compromise with the nationalists. De Gaulle subsequently acquired a progressive reputation in colonial affairs, but this is not visible in his policies as head of the provisional government. In May 1945 a violent demonstration by Algerian nationalists at Sétif was crushed with terrible savagery – an episode de Gaulle hardly mentions in his memoirs. Any progressive inclinations de Gaulle might have had were tempered by his suspicions of the British and Americans. In reality the British were only too happy to see the French re-establish themselves in Indo-China but de Gaulle was slow to see this. Since 1940 his aim had been to bring France out of the war territorially intact: he viewed himself as the trustee of France's interests. This required him to defend the imperial status quo, at least for the moment. Once France had acquired a permanent government again it is possible that de Gaulle, had he still been in power, would have adopted a more flexible position – although his attitude towards the empire while in opposition during the coming years hardly supports this.

De Gaulle's quarrels with Britain and America were unpopular in France – not least with his own Foreign Minister, Georges Bidault. De Gaulle talked of greatness, the population worried more about food; Paul Ramadier, the Minister of Supply, was dubbed Ramadan. The end of the war meant that de Gaulle's de facto dictatorship would soon be over, and that de Gaulle would need to take account of public opinion. In October 1945, parliamentary elections took place. The new assembly was dominated by the three political forces associated in people's minds with the Resistance: the Communists, the Socialists and the newly formed Christian Democrats (MRP). Its most urgent task was to draft a new constitution, and in the meantime it unanimously voted for de Gaulle to remain head of government. But conflicts with him soon arose. The euphoric unanimity of the Liberation period gave way to normal politics. De Gaulle for the first time found himself having to work with an elected assembly and the experience proved distasteful to him.

The irony was that two years earlier de Gaulle himself had helped to rehabilitate the political parties tainted by their association with France's defeat in 1940. During the war some of de Gaulle's followers had advocated setting up a single 'Resistance movement', a sort of Gaullist party. De Gaulle, who at this stage wanted the broadest possible base of support, preferred to admit the former political parties to the CNR alongside the Resistance groups. Thus at the Liberation, the parties could claim a link to the Resistance. Although the parties would have resurfaced anyway, any new movement sponsored by de Gaulle would probably have won a massive majority. But de Gaulle, not wishing to become the leader of a faction, however large, refused to endorse any candidates at the elections. As a result he found himself lacking a political base. Increasingly frustrated by the sniping of the parties in parliament, he took a few days' holiday in January 1946 (his first since 1939) with his family in Antibes. There he read the memoirs of the 17th-century intriguer Cardinal de Retz and pondered his next move. On 20 January, back in Paris, he summoned the cabinet and told them (so he claims): *the exclusive regime of the political parties has returned. I condemn it. But unless I use force to set up a dictatorship, which I do not desire, and which would doubtless come to a bad end, I have no means of preventing this experiment. So I must retire.*

OPPOSITION: 1946-1953

If de Gaulle had expected to be quickly called back by a popular groundswell of support, he was wrong: the French learned to live without him. By abandoning power so abruptly de Gaulle missed his opportunity to shape the form of the constitution that was being drafted. In retrospect this looks like a grave error, given that constitutional issues were soon to become one of his main preoccupations, but at the end of 1945, though he knew what he did not like, his ideas on the subject had still not crystallized.

The constitution proposed by the constituent assembly was rejected in a referendum in May 1946. New elections took place for a fresh assembly but de Gaulle played no part in them. Only following the elections, after five months of silence, did he make a speech at Bayeux, on 16 June 1946 (two years after his return to France) outlining his constitutional proposals. This Bayeux speech is as fundamental to what could be called the second period of Gaullism as that of 18 June 1940 was to the first. In contrast to the parliamentary regime of the Third Republic, with a weak executive at the mercy of fleeting parliamentary majorities, de Gaulle advocated a presidential regime with a head of state *standing above the parties, elected by a college including parliament but wider than it*. It was clear whom de Gaulle had in mind for this post. These ideas were completely alien to France's Republican tradition, which had been forged in the 19th century in opposition to Bonapartism. The assembly rejected the presidential model and drafted a constitution not so different from that of the Third Republic, whose president had been largely a figurehead.

Louis Napoleon Bonaparte (1808-1873), great-nephew of the first Emperor Napoleon, became the living incarnation of the Napoleonic legend after the death of Napoleon's son in 1832. Elected as President of the Second Republic in 1848, he seized power and declared himself Emperor Napoleon III on 2 December 1852 (the anniversary of the coronation of the First Napoleon in 1804 and of the Battle of Austerlitz in 1805). Although Louis Napoleon's style of leadership was authoritarian, it also contained a genuinely democratic dimension. There were periodic plebiscites in which the entire adult male population over 21 had the right to vote. This mixture of democratic populism and charismatic authoritarian leadership came to be dubbed 'Bonapartism'. The experience of Louis Napoleon's seizure of power made French republicans extremely wary of strong and charismatic leaders, an attitude that persisted into the 1960s.

This time the proposed constitution was ratified by the electorate, but only a minority (35 per cent) voted 'yes' (33 per cent voted 'no' and 32 per cent abstained). The Fourth Republic, born in apathy, was soon afflicted by the same instability as its predecessor: the average duration of a government was ten months.

Having failed to bring about the constitution he wanted, in April 1947 de Gaulle founded a party to advance his proposals: the Gathering *(Rassemblement)* of the French People (RPF). Refusing to call the RPF a 'party', de Gaulle wanted it to be a 'movement' appealing across the political spectrum. Inevitably it became a party, even if it had 'objectives' not 'manifestos', 'assizes' not 'congresses', and 'companions' not 'members'. The term 'companion' recalled the Resistance, and many who had followed de Gaulle during the war joined his new movement. The chief organizer was the former anthropologist Jacques Soustelle who had run de Gaulle's wartime intelligence service in Algiers. Another leading member was the novelist André Malraux, a former participant in the internal resistance, who met de Gaulle in 1945 and saw him as a heroic individual worthy of his own fiction. The esteem was mutual.

Most people were dazzled by Malraux but could understand little he said. De Gaulle felt that he had encountered a worthy interlocutor: 'Napoleon meets Goethe', commented one observer. Malraux ran the RPF's propaganda, stage-managing theatrical rallies at which de Gaulle addressed huge crowds.

At the municipal elections of October 1947 the newly launched RPF erupted on to the political scene winning 38.7 per cent of the vote (in second place came the PCF with 28.9 per cent) and capturing control of 13 of the 25 largest cities in France, including Paris. By the spring of 1948 it had about 400,000 members, making it France's second largest party after the PCF. This extraordinary success was largely due to the beginning of the Cold War. In February 1948 the Communists seized power in Prague; in France they launched a series of massive strikes. War seemed imminent in Europe, revolution conceivable in France. In this atmosphere de Gaulle appeared as a bulwark and a saviour. Polls show that the peak of his success correlated exactly with the moment at which people most feared war. His speeches in these years are variations on a theme of catastrophe – apocalyptic visions of inflation, monetary collapse, disintegration of the empire – but above all the threat of Communism. De Gaulle reminded his listeners that the western border of the Soviet bloc was *hardly two stages of the Tour de France* away from France's eastern frontier. He warned darkly that the Russian invaders would be assisted by the French Communists whom de

Anti-Communist pro-Gaullist poster, 1949, warning against descent into civil war in France

Gaulle in this period referred to as 'separatists' because he considered them outside the national political community.

This was the most pro-American period of de Gaulle's career: he welcomed Marshall Aid and the setting up of NATO (1949). But, from 1950, although still resolutely anti-Communist, he became increasingly concerned about the structure of the NATO Alliance, especially the prospect of France's national security being drawn *into a system run by others* (21 October 1950) – in other words, America. By 1952 he came near to putting the dangers of *Soviet slavery* or *an American protectorate* on the same footing (23 May 1952). His growing suspicion of America was fuelled in 1953 by American backing for the projected European Defence Community (EDC) which was a means of selling German rearmament to public opinion. De Gaulle fulminated against this *military Babel, stateless army, monstrosity* under American control.

Whatever de Gaulle's evolving perception of the dangers facing France, one theme was constant: the *impotent* and *infirm* Fourth Republic was incapable of dealing with them: France needed a *State which is a State with a head of State who is a head of State*. In short: *the whole problem of France is dominated by the question of the regime* (16 March 1950). De Gaulle's problem was that in 1947 he had won the wrong election: municipal elections did not bring parliamentary seats. His only hope was that one of the existing groups in parliament would rally to him and force an early election. The MRP, which at the Liberation had presented itself as the party faithful to de Gaulle, was the only group that might have done this. Instead it opted to defend the regime in coalition with the Socialists. This was the so-called 'Third Force' solution – the other two 'forces' being de Gaulle's RPF and the Communists. De Gaulle's success in the municipal elections had helped to consolidate the regime he wanted to end: only fear of de Gaulle (and the Communists) bound the MRP and Socialists together between 1947 and 1951. The President of the Republic, the venerable

Socialist leader Vincent Auriol, may not have had much power, but he vowed that he would not play in France the role of President Hindenburg in Germany, who had appointed Hitler as Chancellor. That such a comparison could be made showed how de Gaulle was viewed in certain circles at this time. De Gaulle hurled imprecations at his opponents: Communism, he said, was the enemy, the Third Force a reincarnation of Vichy, the RPF a new resistance. But the 'treason' of the MRP, as de Gaulle called it, reduced him to impotence until the parliamentary elections of 1951.

De Gaulle threw himself into the election campaign, making 50 speeches in 18 days. The RPF emerged as the largest parliamentary group (120 seats) but not large enough to paralyse the system. This relatively poor result was partly due to a manipulation of the electoral system designed to weaken the RPF and the

De Gaulle as depicted in a 1950 anti-government cartoon by Micou issued by Le Parti Communiste Français attacking the cost of armaments and the Atlantic Pact

PCF. Even so the RPF's share of the vote had fallen to 22.3 per cent. According to de Gaulle this still made it the largest *French* grouping – since only the 'separatist' Communists had won more votes – but it represented a considerable drop since 1947. The truth was that the world no longer seemed so threatening in 1951. The insurrectionary strikes of 1947–8 had been crushed; despite inflation, the economy was recovering thanks to Marshall Aid. De Gaulle denied that any of this improvement was due to a *regime which floats on the nation like scum on the sea* (21 October 1950) and continued to employ the language of catastrophe: *France is under threat, the country is on the verge of a financial abyss* (23 February 1952). But this no longer carried conviction. The terrified bourgeoisie that had rallied to de Gaulle in 1947 no longer needed him: an American protectorate in 1951, if that is what it was, seemed less alarming than a Soviet invasion four years before.

The RPF had too few members of parliament to be able to impose de Gaulle's ideas about reforming the constitution. De Gaulle therefore wanted them to filibuster and refuse cooperation, but some RPF deputies were not attracted by such a thankless role. By 1951 the Third Force had collapsed – itself a sign that de Gaulle no longer frightened people – and one possible alternative was a return of the right to power (for the first time since the Liberation). But this would require the parliamentary support of the RPF. In June 1952 Jacques Soustelle, leader of the RPF's parliamentary group, allowed himself to be sounded out about forming a government. At the governing council of the RPF, de Gaulle unleashed his most ferocious sarcasm: *can we begin while the prime minister forms his government? Where will he put me I wonder? Minister of Sport, or perhaps Under-Secretary of State for Fine Arts?* Soustelle arrived: *Ah, here is the new premier. Well, Mr Prime Minister, how are your consultations going?*[21] By the end Soustelle was on the verge of tears. In fact Soustelle had resisted the temptations of office. But a few weeks later the conservative Antoine Pinay became premier thanks to the votes of 27 dissident RPF deputies; by the end of 1952 45 deputies had broken with the movement. In May 1953 de Gaulle drew the inevitable conclusion: he gave the RPF deputies a free hand in the future but washed his hands of any responsibility for them. The RPF was effectively wound up a year later.

The RPF period is embarrassing for de Gaulle's admirers. Some people have seen the movement as semi-fascist. Claude Mauriac, though he remained faithful to de Gaulle, found the theatrical mass meetings distasteful: he was reminded of the anti-parliamentary Leagues of the 1930s. The RPF stewards used extremely rough methods against hecklers and opponents: at Grenoble in September 1948 a Communist protestor was killed during violent scuffles at an RPF meeting. De Gaulle's speeches in these years were both incendiary and reactionary. Apart from virulent anti-Communism and uncompromising defence of the empire, he took up the theme of an 'association' of capital and labour. This was the major social policy of the RPF, and hardly a speech went by without de Gaulle mentioning it. Exactly what it entailed was obscure: it was supposed to abolish class conflict and involved the 'depoliticization' of the trade unions. At best this was woolly paternalism; at worst a sort of corporatism of the kind favoured by fascist regimes, in which trade unions are abolished in the name of class reconciliation. It is no coincidence that de Gaulle's memoirs, started at this time, pay a curious tribute (the only one they pay) to Vichy's corporatist legislation. De Gaulle also denounced excessive public expenditure and on one occasion envisaged the denationalization of some of those companies he had himself nationalized at the Liberation. On a few occasions in this period de Gaulle, at least in private, mused whether an authoritarian regime was not the only possible defence against Communism in France.[22]

Much of this rhetoric was influenced by the ambient Cold War atmosphere. The Third Force coalition was scarcely less anti-Communist in its policies than de Gaulle in his speeches. As for the idea of the association of capital and labour, although it could be interpreted in a sinister fashion, it was in fact most popular with the left-wing Gaullists. However inflammatory de Gaulle's rhetoric at times, he never seriously called into question the commitment to democracy that he had inherited from the war. Malraux remarked: 'De Gaulle took us to the Rubicon and then told us to take out our fishing rods.' At no time did de Gaulle seriously contemplate a coup: *A pronunciamento? As in Guatemala? That solves nothing, unless it has general consent.*[23] Such statements were a pragmatic recognition of the fact that the conditions for a coup did not exist; and an oblique tribute to democracy as the only source of durable authority. As de Gaulle said some years later to Alain Peyrefitte, his Minister of Information in the Fifth Republic: *it is not that I like the Republic as the Republic, but since the French support it, one has to support it. They cannot imagine living except in a Republic.*[24] To those who accused him of being a potential dictator he would protest: *did I not restore democracy in 1945?*

De Gaulle devoted only a few lines to the RPF in his *Memoirs.* The movement did have some tactical successes – for example in helping to defeat the proposed EDC. It also created a group of Gaullist political cadres who were to become the ruling elite of the Fifth Republic: the war created Gaullism as a legend; the RPF period laid the foundations of it as an organization. These were also years of political apprenticeship for de Gaulle. Between 1940 and 1946 his experience had been primarily diplomatic and military. He had negotiated with Churchill and Stalin; he had outwitted Giraud. But the game of democratic politics remained a closed book to him. In 1946 he had resigned rather than be constrained by its rules and by pygmy politicians; between 1947 and 1955 he was pitting himself against the politicians and lost to the superior political skills of Auriol, Pinay and others. But de Gaulle learnt from the experience: in 1958, exploiting a political crisis to engineer his return to power, he was to outmanoeuvre the politicians brilliantly.

None of this disguises the fact that in the short term the RPF was a failure and that for de Gaulle these were years of bitter impotence. His public and private utterances were drenched in contempt for those who were blocking his return to power. He had an almost infinite register of largely untranslatable –

1951 Communist poster accusing de Gaulle of being an anti-republican and fascist

and sometimes unprintable – epithets for the politicians of the Fourth Republic: the *vinegar pissers*, the *polis-petits-chiens* [well-bred little puppy dogs], *'politichiens', I spew these people up, I despise them beyond words. I don't detest them. One cannot detest nothingness.* This rage was born of frustration: *I did not do what I did on 18 June to bring M. Pinay into power.*[25] But Monsieur Pinay, and others like him, were in power.

THE WAR MEMOIRS I:
INVENTING 'DE GAULLE': 1953–1958

After 1953 de Gaulle gradually withdrew from politics. At a press conference in May 1955, for the second time in his career, he announced his retirement from public affairs: *it will be a long time before we meet again.* He took no part in the elections of 1956. Between 1954 and 1958, apart from four foreign trips, he devoted

De Gaulle took literature very seriously. Writers were the only group to whom he was consistently deferential; every author sending him a work was guaranteed a stately letter thanking the *cher maître* (dear master) in question. Soon after arriving at Algiers in June 1943 de Gaulle invited André Gide to dinner. One of the first people he chose to receive in liberated Paris was the novelist François Mauriac. Having prepared himself mentally for a conversation about politics, Mauriac was amazed to discover that de Gaulle wanted to talk only about literary matters: Gide and the *Académie Française*. Despite Mauriac's intervention a few weeks after their meeting, de Gaulle refused to commute the death sentence on the fascist collaborationist writer Robert Brasillach: literature was too important. De Gaulle wrote of the affair: *in literature as in everything else talent is a bond of responsibility.* The same instinct led him to oppose those who in 1960 wanted him to arrest Sartre for inciting soldiers to desert during the Algerian war: *one does not arrest Voltaire.* As well as taking writers seriously, de Gaulle took himself very seriously as a writer, and spent hours refining his manuscript. He sent the first four dedicated copies of the first volume of his *War Memoirs* to the Pope, the Comte de Paris (the monarchist pretender to the throne of France), the President of the Republic and the Queen of England – in that order. The list reveals much about de Gaulle's sense of hierarchies.

himself to his three volumes of *War Memoirs: The Call (1940–2),* published in 1954, *Unity* (1942–4), published in 1956, and *Salvation (1944–6),* published in 1959.

The *Memoirs* had an explicit political purpose: they kept de Gaulle in the public eye and constructed his image of himself as a figure of destiny. De Gaulle frequently refers to himself in the third person, as Caesar did in his memoirs. 'De Gaulle' appears for the first time on the 71st page, during the description of the fall of France. But de Gaulle later told one of his biographers that it was in October 1940, when arriving at Doula in French Equatorial Africa, that he first became aware of a 'de Gaulle' who existed to some extent outside himself: *There were shouts of 'de Gaulle, de Gaulle.' I was taken aback . . . I realized then that General de Gaulle had become a living legend, that they had formed a certain image of him. Until then in London my contacts had all been personal and individual with ministers, attachés, soldiers and so on. But here was the people, the voice of the crowds . . . There was a person named de Gaulle who existed in other people's minds and was really a separate personality from myself. From that day on I would have to reckon with this man, this General de Gaulle . . . I became almost his prisoner.*[26]

To be this historical 'de Gaulle' is described as *a permanent obligation . . . a permanent inner discipline, a heavy yoke.* Or as he put it on another occasion: *there is one fact that they refuse to take into account . . . that fact is de Gaulle. I don't understand it very well myself but I am a prisoner of it.*[27] He had become a *character from a fable . . . on whom people rely to carry out by himself all the expected miracles.* During the course of the *Memoirs* 'de Gaulle' becomes an ever more insistent presence: he appears 50 times in the first volume, 100 times in the second, 20 times in just the last two chapters of the final volume.

De Gaulle often returned to the idea that, if he had re-created France between 1940 and 1944, in the same period France also created him – as previously it had created Joan of Arc, Georges Clemenceau and others. De Gaulle was *an instrument of destiny*, as much acted upon by history as acting upon it. From this he derived his conviction that his action during the war had conferred upon him a kind of continuing historical legitimacy. In a speech in 1960, he talked of the *national legitimacy I have incarnated for twenty years* – an astonishing claim for someone who for 12 of those years had been leader of an unsuccessful opposition party. His resignation in 1946 was partly motivated by the desire to preserve intact his latent moral capital: a figure of destiny could not allow himself to be trapped by Lilliputian politicians. As he remarked at the time to one astonished politician: *Can one imagine Joan of Arc married, a mother, perhaps even deceived by her husband?*[28] When, soon after his resignation, the government wanted to offer de Gaulle some kind of decoration, he was scornful: *they simply do not understand the absolutely unique and exceptional nature of the Odyssey from 1940 to the Liberation which had no precedent in history . . . The poor fools . . . I am no mere victorious general. One does not decorate France.*[29] In a similar spirit, de Gaulle distinguished his own historical achievement from that of Clemenceau, who had led France to victory in World War One: *I see an essential difference between Clemenceau's epic and my own. Clemenceau never gave rise to a mystique. He was a great historical actor . . . who brought us victory, he was the fact of victory; while I, on the other hand, was swept forward by the great historical force I had brought about, and which represented infinitely more than my person.*[30]

If the third person 'de Gaulle' was partly a creation of history, outside de Gaulle's control, he was also a self-creation. Before 1940 de Gaulle had reflected at length on the nature of leadership, most explicitly in his book *The Edge of the Sword*. The events of 1940 provided the stage, but de Gaulle had already written the script. 'De Gaulle' is therefore also an actor playing out a long-meditated role. The metaphor of the stage recurs frequently in de Gaulle's writings: three chapters of the *War Memoirs* are consecutively entitled 'Interlude', 'Tragedy', 'Comedy'.

Leadership for de Gaulle was a kind of creative instinct, but also a performance. Leadership had to be developed consciously, and practised: *the leader, like the artist, must have an inborn propensity which can be strengthened by the exercise of his craft.*[31] Thus Churchill was *an exceptional artist, the great artist of a great history.* The leader needs to cultivate authority and prestige by keeping distance, by creating mystery and surprise through silence. The chaplain of de Gaulle's regiment, asking in 1940 why de Gaulle was so solitary and so silent, was told: *solitude, silence, reflection, you know better than me: without them, what would words achieve, even the word of God? All those who have achieved something valuable and lasting have been silent and solitary people.*[32] It was silence that gave words their greatest resonance, their most dramatic impact. In de Gaulle's view, Napoleon was lost once he ceased to surprise. There was a degree of calculated showmanship in de Gaulle's tantrums against the British, and in his surprise resignation in 1946. As he commented a few days after this resignation: *In leaving without looking back, I kept my air of mystery.*[33]

In de Gaulle's conception of leadership the leader is always watching himself. In *The Edge of the Sword* de Gaulle argues that the self-discipline necessary for leadership leads to an *intimate struggle, more or less intense according to the individual, but which does not fail at every moment to wound his soul as the flint tears the feet of the penitent sinner.* The leader is condemned to melancholy solitude: *what people agree to call happiness* (a favourite phrase) is incompatible with leadership. Already in the notebooks he kept as a World War One prisoner we find de Gaulle writing in a similar vein: *self-mastery must become a sort of habit, a moral reflex created by a constant exercise of the will, especially in small things: dress, conversation, thought, a method worked out and applied in everything, particularly one's work.*[34]

How flinty for Charles de Gaulle was the path that led to being 'de Gaulle'? The memoirs do not tell us. They reveal nothing directly of the inner man. But it does seem that the distance and separateness that he imposed on himself came naturally to him. This may have come partly from a sense of physical awkwardness: describing his parade down the Champs Elysées in 1944 de Gaulle comments that he had *neither the physique nor the taste for those attitudes and gestures that can please the public.* One of his fellow prisoners in World War One describes how in the enforced promiscuity of prison showers de Gaulle contrived never to be seen naked. Harold Macmillan describes going on a bathing expedition with him in Algeria in 1943: while Macmillan plunged naked into the water, de Gaulle observed from a rock, draped in his uniform and his dignity. To one follower de Gaulle once

The devoted family man, de Gaulle and his wife Yvonne with their daughter and grandchildren

remarked: *we giants are never at ease with others . . . The armchairs are always too small, the tables too low, the impression one makes too strong.*[35] A body too can be tamed, and de Gaulle came to exploit his considerable height (6'5" or 1.96m) as when raising his arms above his head in a huge V. But he always remained awkwardly self-conscious about his appearance. After two cataract operations in the 1950s, he had to wear thick glasses, but he hated to do so in public: could one imagine Joan of Arc in spectacles?

The intimate de Gaulle was confined to his family and remains inaccessible. This separateness was preserved by the existence of Colombey as the family retreat, 200 miles (320 kilometres) from Paris. Family life was important to de Gaulle: as far as circumstances allowed, he and his wife were together for the 49 years of their married life. They had three children – two daughters and one son. The third child, Anne, was born with Down's Syndrome, and died in 1948 at the age of twenty. De Gaulle lavished love on her and was said to be the only person who could make her laugh. He set up a foundation for handicapped children to which he devoted much of the income from his memoirs. At Colombey, the de Gaulles lived the well-regulated existence of a 19th-century bourgeois couple of modest means. The sound of Mme de Gaulle's knitting needles is a backdrop to many accounts of a day spent at Colombey. Jacques Soustelle was always irritated by the stuffy provinciality of the atmosphere; others found it soothing; de Gaulle found it restorative. His distractions were solitary: long walks around the park and endless games of patience. He was punctilious and polite as a host: rudeness was a facet of the public de Gaulle, not the private one. Mme de Gaulle was a prudish Catholic whose only known intervention in politics was to prevent de Gaulle having divorced men as ministers.

De Gaulle's religion was entirely private: although scrupulous in his attendance at mass, he often seemed distracted. Claude Mauriac was startled when during a mass that he had specially arranged for himself de Gaulle pointed out some Allied aeroplanes in the sky outside. De Gaulle once described himself as a Catholic by tradition and geography. France appears on almost every page of his writing, God almost never. He was indifferent to music and to the visual arts. The only sculpture that spoke to him, he told Malraux, was that of the Middle Ages: *it is France . . . The rest is archaeology.* His literary tastes were conventional for someone of his background and generation – Corneille, Racine, Chateaubriand, Rostand, Claudel – but he also enjoyed the novels of Françoise Sagan, a more risqué author; for the subjunctives, so he said.

This life of respectable ordinariness tells us little more about the inner de Gaulle than does his role as heroic leader. His closest advisers all declared it was impossible to achieve intimacy or familiarity with him. It is true that we have abundant record of de Gaulle's private conversation. But his conversation was merely another sort of performance for a more intimate audience. In the end all de Gaulle's talking, as one adviser noted, was with himself; his advisers were mirrors in which he would examine his own ideas.

Many saw de Gaulle's remoteness as coldness. During the war Harold Macmillan described him as 'Ramrod' – 'all the rigidity of a poker without its occasional warmth'. Yet it would be wrong to see de Gaulle as a cold man. Beneath the carapace there was an incredible intensity of feeling, which expressed itself frequently in volcanic eruptions of contempt. Churchill commented that de Gaulle was a man with an extraordinary capacity for suffering. He felt the fall of France in 1940 as a terrible personal humiliation. De Gaulle's hidden passion was partly of course ambition. As de Gaulle wrote to a fellow officer in the 1920s: *promotion is pleasant but the real question is to make one's mark.*[36]

Part of de Gaulle's fabled remoteness was the outward composure of an instinctive risk-taker. The image of the gambler recurs frequently with de Gaulle: *I threw the dice* he wrote of one moment in his quarrel with Giraud. In *The Edge of the Sword* he compares the self-control of the leader to that of the gambler whose *elegance consists in reinforcing his outward appearance of sang-froid at the moment that he takes the winnings.* In *The Edge of the Sword* de Gaulle refers to the *jeu divin du héros,* the divine sport of the hero, the contest which confers nobility on history and interest to life.

De Gaulle's ambition was rescued from irresponsibility or cynicism by his complete identification of France's interests with his own and his own with France. In his eyes his ambition – and ambition was always a positive term for him – had an almost impersonal quality, quite different from Napoleon's, which he described as the 'childish' individual ambition of a vulgar adventurer: *he conceived his destiny as that of an extraordinary individual. But an individual counts for little compared to a nation.*[37]

De Gaulle's sense of serving a cause higher than himself heightened his natural authoritarianism. He was acutely suspicious of others, often unreasonably so – many photographs of de Gaulle show him looking suspiciously out of the corner of his eye – and unforgiving once challenged. There was always about de Gaulle

Pierre Brossolette was a Resistance leader whose vision, intelligence and energy made him the only rival to Jean Moulin. Like Moulin, he was eventually captured and executed by the Germans. He admired what de Gaulle represented politically but this did not blind him to de Gaulle's faults. In the autumn of 1942 he wrote the General a long letter: 'I want to speak frankly to you. I have always done this with the men, however great they might be, whom I respect and like . . . For there are moments when someone must have the courage to say to your face what others are thinking behind your back . . . Your way of treating people . . . is something that worries us a lot. There are subjects on which you do not tolerate any contradiction, not even the slightest debate . . . Your tone makes your interlocutors fear that any dissent on their part could only result from stupidity or a lack of patriotism. There is no doubt a certain greatness in the imperiousness of your manner which leads too many of your collaborators to enter your office with quaking fear . . . but this is also dangerous. It means that the less impressive members of your entourage merely repeat what you want to hear; the worst of them flatter you shamelessly; and you alienate people of real quality . . . This is why I take it upon myself to beg you to make the necessary effort while there is still time . . . You must try and develop more human relationships with those who want to serve you, solicit their opinions, weigh their advice.' Brossolette never received an answer.

something of the army officer who had strayed into politics, inclined to treat disagreement as insubordination. He felt most affinity for those trained for disinterested public service – many of whom became ministers in his Fifth Republic governments – and was more wary of those from less conventional backgrounds. We have already seen how one Resistance member remarked on de Gaulle's apparent massive ingratitude to the Resistance. De Gaulle would have replied that the state (the 'coldest of cold monsters', a favourite phrase from Nietzsche) knows no gratitude: one's duty is to serve it. De Gaulle could inspire extraordinary loyalty, but his superhuman perspective alienated others. One resister, received by de Gaulle in 1945 on returning from imprisonment in

Buchenwald, was startled by de Gaulle's total lack of interest in his prison experiences: de Gaulle was 'above all preoccupied by my future plans and concerned that I return to my Civil Service post.' Although de Gaulle had mellowed somewhat by the end of the 1950s, the change was only one of degree: he had become more affable but no less distant.

THE WAR MEMOIRS II: INVENTING 'GAULLISM'

De Gaulle's *Memoirs*, taken together with his speeches between 1940 and 1955, also delineate the elements of Gaullism as a political doctrine. In fact de Gaulle tended to use the word 'Gaullism' in inverted commas, and he rejected the idea that it was an ideology. But the word is useful to describe the complex of beliefs that by the mid-1950s had crystallized into an exceptionally coherent view of the world and would guide his political action once he returned to power after 1958.

All Gaullism is distilled in the celebrated first paragraph of de Gaulle's *War Memoirs*: *All my life I have had a certain idea of France. It has been inspired as much by sentiment as by reason. The emotional side of me imagines France, like the princess in the fairy stories or the madonna in the frescoes, as dedicated to an exalted and exceptional destiny. Instinctively I have the feeling that Providence has created her for complete successes or exemplary misfortunes. If, in spite of this, mediocrity shows in her acts and deeds, it strikes me as an absurd anomaly imputable to the faults of the French not the genius of the country. But the positive side of my mind also convinces me that France is not really herself except in the front rank [rang]; that only vast enterprises are capable of counterbalancing the ferment of dispersion that our people carries in itself; that our country, such as it is, among others, such as they are, must aim high and hold itself straight, on pain of mortal danger. In short, to my mind, France cannot be France without greatness [grandeur].* The polarities around which this passage is constructed – reason/sentiment, successes/misfortunes, vast enterprises/ferment of dispersion, mediocrity/*grandeur*, front rank/mortal danger, France/the French — shape de Gaulle's history of France into an epic of alternating greatness and decline, in which the interests of the French are not always those of France. It is constantly necessary to be vigilant in France's defence. The memoirs end: *Old France, weighed down by history, bruised by war and revolution, endlessly coming and going between grandeur and decline, but revived century after century, by the genius of renewal.*

Gaullism is built around a vision of what France should be, and a didactic reading of history which explains why she has not always lived up to that vision. The French people have too often been tempted by *mediocrity, renunciation, abandonment* (all favourite words). *The French are cattle*, de Gaulle sometimes remarked in private — especially when they showed signs of disagreeing with him. It could be said of him, as

On 14 July 1943 in Algiers de Gaulle announced: *Our fatherland has existed for 15 centuries — both in its tribulations and its glories.* On other occasions he talked of French history having lasted ten centuries — or 20. Puzzled by these contradictions, Alain Peyrefitte once asked him to explain them. De Gaulle replied: *Twenty centuries, that takes us back to Vercingetorix: he was the first resister of our race. Fifteen centuries, that takes us back to Clovis: in uniting Roman Gaul and Christianity, the King of the Franks was the true creator of France. Ten centuries, that takes us back to Hugues Capet: he installed the dynasty which extended French power from the area around Paris to the whole of the Hexagon.* In de Gaulle's youth it had been an axiom of the monarchist right that French history began with King Clovis, the first King to be baptized Catholic, while the Republicans had dated French history back to the leader of the Gauls, Vercingetorix. De Gaulle, typically, attempts to synthesize these competing French traditions.

Keynes wrote of Clemenceau, that 'he had one illusion — France; and one disillusion — mankind, including Frenchmen'. But for de Gaulle the real weakness of the French people was something in which he took an almost sombre pride: their 'divisions', their 'quarrels', their *eternal demons* of dispersal. These he saw as a national characteristic going back to the Gauls, and accentuated by the legacy of the Revolution. As he once remarked: *How can you govern a country with 265 types of cheese?*[38]

According to de Gaulle, France's divisions could only be overcome by pursuing a policy of national *grandeur* (greatness), and this was only possible when the State was strong. De Gaulle was pragmatic about the best political system to achieve this. He took as his guiding principle Solon's reply when asked to define the best constitution: *for what people and in what period?* (16 June 1946) De Gaulle's answer to that question for the French in the 20th century was that monarchy, for example, was no longer a viable option. Instead he proposed, in his famous Bayeux speech, to transform the Republic by strengthening the executive (the president) at the expense of the legislative (parliament). The disaster of 1940 had occurred because the state had simply disintegrated. As he put it in his Tacitean comment on Lebrun, President of the Third Republic in 1940: *As chief of state, he had lacked two things: he was not a chief, and there was no state.* The state had lost its legitimacy.

The concept of legitimacy was fundamental for de Gaulle. The legitimacy of a regime derived, first of all, from its capacity to preserve national independence, to defend its territory: *no legitimacy without independence* (15 May 1947). In this sense Vichy, although technically legal, was from its origins illegitimate because dependent on Germany. The second condition of legitimacy was popular support: *the profound republican legitimacy which comes from an agreement between the nation and the governing power* (17 April 1948). On both counts de Gaulle viewed the Fourth Republic as illegitimate – he would affect to talk of its 'so-called governments' – for having allowed France to become too dependent on America and for lacking popular support. Only a strong state could guarantee national independence but it could not be strong unless it was rooted in popular support; and the national unity that brings such support is only possible if the state offers the people a policy of national independence and *grandeur.* The three elements – a strong state, national independence, and popular support – are interdependent.

That legitimacy derived from the people was axiomatic for de Gaulle. He always resented accusations that he was an aspirant dictator. To those who accused him during the RPF period of being another Bonaparte, he replied that he opposed dictatorship: *first of all as a matter of principle; I don't need to insist on that. And then because of the realities of France. We have often experimented with it during our history . . . But dictatorship always finishes badly in France* (6 July 1952). De Gaulle's notion of popular sovereignty was essentially plebiscitary. He saw democracy less as a means for the expression of legitimate opposition than as a way of affirming national unity, less as an articulation of the tensions of a pluralistic society than as a ratification of policy. In this context, nothing in his *War Memoirs* is more revealing than the panegyric on unity in his description of the procession down the Champs Elysées in liberated Paris: *Ahead of me the Champs Elysées! Rather the sea! An immense crowd was massed on either side of the street. Perhaps two million people. The roofs too were black with people . . . I went on foot . . . Today we were to revive, by the spectacle of its joy and the evidence of its liberty, the self-awareness of a people who yesterday were crushed by defeat and dispersed in servitude. Since each person there had, in his heart, chosen Charles de Gaulle as refuge against his hurt and symbol of his hope, they must be allowed to see him, familiar and fraternal, so that at this sight national unity should shine forth . . . This was one of those miracles of national consciousness, one of those gestures which sometimes, in the course of centuries, illuminate the history of France. In this community with only a single thought, a single enthusiasm, a single cry, all differences vanished, all individuals disappeared. Innumerable Frenchmen whom I approached first at the Etoile, then at the Rond-Pont, then at the Place de la*

Concorde, before the Hôtel de Ville, on the steps of the cathedral – if you knew how alike you were!

De Gaulle's version of democracy had little time for parties, unions and other intermediary organizations, even if he had to accept them in practice. De Gaulle had an endless list of derogatory epithets for those *elites, clans, castes* which stood between him and *the depths of the nation (la nation profonde).* They were floating on the surface of the nation, to use one favourite image, like scum on the ocean deep. Parties could only represent *particular interests* with their own *clientele.* De Gaulle's hatred of party was visceral: he avoided setting up a Gaullist movement during the war; during 1944 to 1946 he refused to associate himself with any political group; and when he founded a party in 1947 he called it a Gathering *(Rassemblement)* and ditched it in 1953. De Gaulle's contempt for parties was part of his intolerance of disagreement. It also reflected a feeling that the 'notables', the elites, the bourgeoisie, had betrayed France in 1940, and left the population leaderless, vulnerable to the defeatism of Pétain: *my greatest adversary, that of France, has never ceased to be the power of money.*[39] Or as he put it on another occasion: *the bourgeoisie was behind Pétain in 1940 because it wanted no interruption to its dinner parties despite the national disaster.*[40] De Gaulle felt no affinity with the moneyed bourgeoisie; his own personal tastes were modest: *I have never been bourgeois. The bourgeoisie is wealth – the sense of having it or the desire to acquire it. My family and myself have always been poor . . . I have never felt linked to the interests of this class.*[41]

In this context it is worth briefly examining de Gaulle's economic and social ideas. His economic notions were predictably orthodox. His instincts, in spite of his choice of Pleven over Mendès France in 1945, were generally for financial and monetary stability. But although having a traditional approach to financial and economic affairs, de Gaulle was no *laissez-faire* liberal. In 1945 he backed Monnet's idea for the economic planning commissariat which became such a distinctive feature of French economic policy; in the 1960s he famously declared economic planning to be an *ardent necessity*. De Gaulle's belief in a strong state made it easy for him to accept this notion.

His social doctrine, if it can so be described, also distinguished his position from *laissez-faire policy*. In a speech in 1941 he had criticized the way in which mechanization and the growing uniformity of modern civilization crushed individualism. This preoccupation surfaced periodically in his career. De Gaulle's solution to the problem of alienation – his means of restoring the *dignity* of man, as he put it – was a *third way* between socialism and unregulated capitalism. He toyed with the idea that workers should be given a greater role in the running of their firms, or that they should be given some share in the profits. In the RPF period this was described as *association*, in the mid-1960s as *participation*. Because de Gaulle was never interested in the technical details of social policy, these ideas always remained rather woolly – and many Gaullists were very sceptical about them – but as a general aspiration they were very important to him. They were rooted in social Catholic thinking which was influential from the late 19th century in the kind of milieu into which de Gaulle was born. Social Catholics preached various forms of class reconciliation, and sought to show that the Church was not indifferent to social problems raised by industrial capitalism even if they rejected socialist solutions. It is striking that during the 1930s de Gaulle became a subscriber to the progressive Christian Democrat periodical *Temps Présent*. This is an aspect of his thinking which is too often overlooked.

De Gaulle refused to be characterized as either being of left or right – hence his famous remark, *everyone is, has been or will be Gaullist*. Gaullism was to some extent a successful synthesis of French traditions. As de Gaulle himself said, *The problem in France is that the right is against the nation and the left detests the State*.[42] De

Gaulle was genuinely unconcerned by the political origins of those who were ready to work for the interests of France. As he commented of the Communist leader Thorez, who served in his post-war government: *while making every effort to advance the interests of Communism, he was to serve the public interest on several occasions. Was this out of patriotic instinct or political opportunism? It was not my job to unravel his motives. It sufficed that the State was served.* (Though it should be added that de Gaulle made sure that the Communists never controlled any portfolios relating to defence, foreign affairs or internal security.)

There are obvious similarities between Gaullism and Bonapartism. Napoleon and de Gaulle shared a similar hatred of parties, a cult of heroic leadership, the practice of plebiscitary democracy, and a socially progressive rhetoric. But, even if Gaullism is just one manifestation of a political sensibility that recurs often in French history, Bonapartism was never a point of reference or an inspiration for de Gaulle, who despised the vulgarity of the Second Empire.

Other commentators have claimed that de Gaulle's political ideas owe a lot to the nationalist writer Charles Maurras. Although, as we have seen, de Gaulle quickly parted company with Maurras's reading of French history, his influence is perceptible in other ways. De Gaulle's distinction between *la nation profonde* and the regime is reminiscent of Maurras's between the '*pays réel*' and the '*pays légal*' – between, as he saw it, the 'reality' of the nation and the 'legal' Republic artificially imposed upon it. De Gaulle's ideas on carving up Germany in the late 1940s were entirely in the *Action Française* tradition. Above all de Gaulle's debt to Maurras is clear in his emphasis on the need for a strong executive authority. De Gaulle's presidency, and the rationale for it, was in a sense a democratized and republicanized version of Maurras's monarch.

Gaullism cannot be reduced to one source, however. It was

forged out of the coming together of an unusual temperament, a certain cast of mind and a set of historical circumstances. De Gaulle was a highly educated man, a lover of Chateaubriand and Corneille, influenced by the pragmatism of Bergson, steeped in the mystical and romantic nationalism of Barrès and Péguy as well as the classical nationalism of Maurras, sympathetic to social Christianity and to the ideas of Marshal Lyautey on the social role of the officer, familiar also with the writings of Nietzsche, Machiavelli and Clausewitz, and aware of the debates which had taken place in the 1930s on the reform of the State. These influences largely situate de Gaulle's intellectual origins on the right. In the 1940s, if he was not an anti-Republican in the style of Maurras, he was no great lover of the Republic either. He was at best a *republicain de raison* not *de coeur* – a republican of the head, not the heart. Between 1940 and 1944 the 'people' enter into de Gaulle's vision of things. In 1944 he actually met them on the Champs Elysées. But although the debility of the French state had preoccupied him at least since 1940, de Gaulle's constitutional ideas were extremely vague before 1946. It was his experience as head of the provisional government after 1944 that crystallized his contempt for political parties and clarified his constitutional programme. From this point onwards his thought was more or less set. If, then, one takes the key elements of Gaullism as a certain vision of France, the people as the source of legitimacy, and the need for a strong state, one could say crudely that de Gaulle was brought up with the first, discovered the second between 1940 and 1944, and learnt how to implement the third by 1946.

In the end de Gaulle should be judged as a man of action rather than an original thinker. It is less revealing to analyse his thought than to highlight certain favourite positive and negative words which recur in his writings. De Gaulle's discourse was constructed around a highly personal vocabulary of polarities, the reflection of a Manichean view of the world (he was never a good negotiator) and of a mercurial temperament:

NEGATIVE	POSITIVE
Decadence, mediocrity	Rank, *grandeur*
Servitude, impotence	Independence
Notables, elites	People, *la nation profonde*
Gentle	Hard, harsh (*rude*)
Abandonment, renunciation	Ambition, dreams, effort
Abyss	Summits
Small	Vast, immense
Clans, parties, factions, fiefs, committees	Unity, *rassemblement*
Disorder, division	Cohesion, order

Some of these polarities are not so surprising, but, taken together, de Gaulle's keywords help us to plot the contours of his mind. The de Gaulle who in 1932 exhorted the military to *lift up its head and look to the summits* is recognizably the ancestor of the man who in 1959 declared that *the road that I offer is hard [rude], but it rises to the summits* or that *with the departure of de Gaulle, gone was that wind from the summits, that hope of success, that ambition for France.* These verbal echoes testify to an underlying consistency to de Gaulle's life and thought. He was imbued with a particular vision of France's history that allowed him to place the events of the present and the future in a long historical pattern. In July 1943 he told Roosevelt's representative: *you have been in France for twelve years. I have lived here for two thousand already.* Coming out of a cabinet meeting in the 1960s, he was heard to mutter, *I have been saying it for a thousand years.*[43] One civil servant who went to talk to him in 1958 about Algeria received an historical lecture which began with the Visigoths.[44] De Gaulle liked to remark that Colombey stood near the site of the Battle of the Cataulaunian Fields where Attila the Hun had been defeated in 450.

For de Gaulle nothing seemed new. The cycle of events that he had lived through between 1940 and 1944 was like a condensed version of that history of light and shade, *grandeur* and decline, that was, in his view, the characteristic of France's history since the Gauls, and, indeed was a repetition of the cycle that he had personally experienced between 1890 and 1918: from the sad shadow of defeat by Germany in 1870 to the victory of World War One. Common to both cycles were those moments of national euphoria – the 'Sacred Union' of 1914, the procession down the Champs Elysées of 1944 – in which civil strife briefly gave way to national unanimity. Gaullism was about re-creating those fleeting moments, those 'miracles of national consciousness', in which the boy born into a monarchist and Catholic family in an anti-clerical Republic discovered the sense of his existence.

Power: 1958–1969

RETURN TO POWER: MAY 1958

The third volume of de Gaulle's *War Memoirs* ends with de Gaulle apostrophizing himself: *Old man exhausted by ordeals, detached from human deeds, feeling the approach of the eternal cold, but never weary of watching in the shadows for the gleam of hope*. By the time these words were published the 'old man' was already back in power, but during what Gaullists like to call 'the crossing of the desert', between 1955 and 1958, the gleam of hope looked dim indeed. An opinion poll in 1953 showed that only 1 per cent of the electorate wanted de Gaulle to return to power. Despite moments of optimism, encouraged by the rapturous reception he received on foreign trips, de Gaulle's mood fluctuated violently. In moments of despair he viewed his career as a series of failures: imprisonment in World War One; failure to convert the military to his ideas in the 1930s; the disastrous mission to Dakar in September 1940; and the RPF years after 1946. He toyed with the idea of giving up – as he had for instance after the Dakar expedition. These bouts of pessimism have been incorporated into the Gaullist myth – the man of destiny who overcomes the temptation of solitude (*solitude was my temptation. Now she has become my friend*) – but the temptation was part of de Gaulle's cyclothymic temperament, oscillating between action and withdrawal.

In the 1950s his sense of ageing heightened his frustration: as he remarked famously of Pétain, *old age is a shipwreck. I am a poor old man who is losing his sight*, he told a correspondent in 1955.[45] By 1957 he indeed seemed an old man to those who met him: he was heavier and moved less easily. But his memory remained extraordinary, and although his *War Memoirs* painted the picture of a hermit in bucolic exile at Colombey, he kept in touch with events through weekly visits to Paris, and through information provided by his political lieutenant, Olivier Guichard. Meanwhile he disguised his frustration in black humour: *the regime will lose the Sahara! It'll lose Alsace! We'll only be left with the Auvergne because no one will want it.*[46] The bleak landscapes of Colombey suited his mood at this time. One visitor was told *you can see it is not very gay here . . . one does not come here to amuse oneself.*[47]

From 1957, however, events started to move in de Gaulle's favour. In Algeria a nationalist uprising in 1954 was developing into a full-scale war. The conflict began to poison French politics. Political parties became divided between diehard supporters of *Algérie française* and those favouring negotiation with the rebel FLN. Any suggestion by the French government that it might seek a compromise with the FLN caused outrage among the *pieds noirs.* Between November 1957 and April 1958 the issue toppled two governments. A number of leading politicians came to feel privately that only de Gaulle could resolve this tangled and explosive situation. In March 1958 a leading political commentator wrote an article in the *Le Monde* newspaper entitled 'When?' – asking when, not if, de Gaulle would return. Opinion polls also registered de Gaulle's renewed popularity: a survey of public opinion in January 1958 showed more people had confidence in him to solve the Algerian problem than in any other politician. But de Gaulle was out of power, and it was not clear how he could return to power, since he had supposedly abandoned active politics. At his valedictory press conference in May 1955 de Gaulle had said that only a catastrophe would bring him back. Three years later the catastrophe came – from Algiers.

In Algeria the *pieds noirs* and the army were being driven to adopt ever more extreme positions by their fear that Paris was preparing to betray the cause of *Algérie française.* Neither group was particularly pro-Gaullist: the army doubted de Gaulle's

Algeria had been a French possession since 1830. Its situation was different from other French colonies for two reasons. Firstly, it was administered as part of France itself: diehard colonialists used to say that the Mediterranean ran through France like the river Seine through Paris. Secondly, there was a large population of European settlers: about 1 million Europeans to 9 million indigenous Muslims. Many of these Europeans – known as *pieds noirs* (black feet), allegedly because when they first arrived in Algeria in the 19th century their black boots distinguished them from the barefoot local population – had been in Algeria for generations and felt they had as much right to be in Algeria as anyone else. They believed in what they called *Algérie française* (French Algeria) and ideally wanted the total integration of Algeria into France.

But this did not mean that they were ready to grant full political rights to the Muslim majority, and they sabotaged all French government attempts to persuade them to do so. The *pieds noirs'* refusal to give up any of their privileges stoked a radical independence movement among the Muslims. On 1 November 1954 a group calling itself the National Liberation Front (FLN) launched a coordinated series of terrorist attacks on the Europeans. The Paris government sent the army to smash the FLN, but the violence only escalated over the next three years. Many of the professional army officers had witnessed at first hand the defeat of France in Indo-China, and they came to see victory in Algeria as a way of redeeming their honour. Thus, for different reasons, they identified as fiercely as the *pieds noirs* with *Algérie française.*

commitment to *Algérie française*; many *pieds noirs* were former Pétainists. But there were Gaullist activists in Algiers, such as the former RPF organizer Léon Delebecque, working to channel discontent into support for de Gaulle. As for de Gaulle himself, he kept informed but not directly involved. When Delebecque asked how he would greet a rising in Algeria in his name, de Gaulle replied gnomically that he would *know how to assume his responsibilities*.

The drama broke on 13 May when, after a prolonged ministerial crisis, the new government of Pierre Pflimlin, a liberal over

Algeria, appeared before parliament for the first time. In Algiers demonstrators stormed the government buildings and formed a 'Committee of Public Safety'. General Jacques Massu, commander of the paratroopers and a Gaullist, had himself declared president. The army had turned a riot into an insurrection, and demanded a 'Government of Public Safety' in Paris. The enterprising Delebecque got himself on to the Algiers Committee and it was at his prompting that, on 15 May, General Raoul Salan, army commander-in-chief in Algeria, ended a speech: 'Vive de Gaulle!' (Long live de Gaulle!) The arrival of de Gaulle's long-term associate Jacques Soustelle, a fervent supporter of *Algérie française*, further helped to swing the mood towards de Gaulle. The government in Paris had lost control of Algiers and could not even count on the loyalty of the army in France.

On 15 May, de Gaulle – in the first of three brilliantly calculated interventions – issued a seven-line communiqué condemning the *degradation of the state* and announcing his readiness *to assume the Powers of the Republic*. This statement transformed the situation: by proposing himself as a candidate for power, de Gaulle encouraged the putschists and sabotaged any possible compromise between government and army. As one historian put it: 'there were now not merely two rival sources of power but three: legal, actual, moral: Paris, Algiers, Colombey'.[48] Could a peaceful transition from one to another be effected? De Gaulle had no desire to play Franco, but his communiqué had alarmed the politicians whose support he needed for any legal return to power. On 19 May, therefore, he held a press conference – his second intervention – to reassure them. The communiqué of 15 May was addressed to Algiers, the press conference to Paris.

The press conference was a great event, de Gaulle's first public performance for three years. He recalled that he had re-established the Republic in 1944: *do you think at 67 I am going to start a career as dictator?* But he also avoided condemning the army, whose

Big pied noir demonstration in Algiers, May 13 1958

action he attributed to frustration with the weakness of the state rather than a desire for *Algérie française* – about which he said nothing. He also spoke warmly of the Socialist leader, Guy Mollet, remembering fondly a non-existent meeting they had had in 1944: a parliamentary return to power would require Socialist support.

This skilful performance began the process of dissolving the opposition to de Gaulle. Leading politicians put out feelers. First to visit Colombey, on 22 May, was Pinay, one of France's leading conservative politicians, who was given tea and returned charmed. The effects of de Gaulle's charm were supplemented by those of fear. On 24 May paratroopers from Algiers landed in Corsica and the army in Algiers drew up plans for a landing in France – code-named 'Resurrection' – if a satisfactory political solution should not emerge. With this prospect in sight, Mollet and another leading Socialist, Vincent Auriol, both wrote to de

Gaulle. But all these politicians – Auriol, Mollet, Pinay – required a condemnation of the army before committing themselves to him. Paris was moving. But so was Algiers: on 26 May de Gaulle received a nervous letter from Salan warning that he could not contain the situation indefinitely.

De Gaulle therefore decided, as he put it later, *to accelerate the progress of good sense* – that is, his return to power. He summoned Prime Minister Pflimlin to a secret meeting at midnight on 26 May. Although amicable, the meeting produced no progress, since Pflimlin asked for a condemnation of events in Algiers and de Gaulle refused, making the valid point that he could only do this once. If he condemned the army but there was no resolution of the political situation, de Gaulle would have exhausted his capital with the military. After his meeting with Pflimlin, de Gaulle issued a communiqué (27 May) announcing that he had begun the *regular process* of forming a government and therefore appealed for order in Algiers. This was the most audacious of his three interventions: for the first time he implicitly condemned events in Algiers (to reassure the politicians) but on the grounds that he was forming a government (to reassure the army). Since Pflimlin

was still premier this was simply bluff. Up to a point it worked. Pflimlin, though outraged by de Gaulle's initiative, resigned on 28 May. But his parliamentary majority remained intact. Furthermore, de Gaulle's communiqué hardened the

Putschist Generals: Salan and Massu in Algiers, May 14 1958

Socialists' opposition to him. All but three voted on 27 May 'in no circumstances' to accept his return to power.

President René Coty, who had lost faith in the Republic over which he presided, now played a key role. He arranged a secret meeting on 28 May between de Gaulle and the Speakers of the Senate and Chamber, Gaston Monnerville and André Le Troquer, hoping that they could effect an arrangement with the politicians. The meeting failed because de Gaulle would not compromise on the terms of his return: the drafting of a new constitution to be submitted to referendum. After this failure, Coty spent a sleepless night, and then issued a message (29 May) that he was calling upon 'the most illustrious of Frenchmen' to form a government, and threatening to resign if this should fail. On the next day de Gaulle began to form a government. He received Mollet and Auriol, both of whom he charmed. Mollet returned from Colombey under the spell: 'I have experienced one of the greatest moments of my life.' The Socialists' scruples were weakened when, on 29 May, de Gaulle published his reply to Auriol's letter to him. In it de Gaulle reaffirmed his democratic credentials: *I could not consent to receive power from any other source than the people or their representatives.*

On 1 June de Gaulle's government was voted into power by 329 votes to 224 (42 Socialists voted for, 49 against), despite the opposition of important figures like Mendès France and François Mitterrand. De Gaulle was granted authority to draft a new constitution and parliament went into recess. De Gaulle's political finesse in these two weeks had been extraordinary. Of course other figures played a role as well: Massu, Soustelle and Delebecque in focussing Algerian hopes on de Gaulle; Auriol and Mollet in selling de Gaulle to the Socialists; Coty in breaking the deadlock by asking de Gaulle to form a government; and de Gaulle's indefatigable assistant Guichard in weaving contacts with the politicians.

But ultimately the victory was de Gaulle's. He managed

through a masterly combination of seduction, bluff and firmness to impose his rhythm on events. He played Paris against Algiers and the politicians against the army, while refusing to be tied down by either.

Yet the question remains: if de Gaulle had not succeeded in returning to power legally, would he have given the go-ahead for 'Resurrection'? De Gaulle's closest collaborators kept themselves fully informed of the military preparations for the invasion. On 28 May, at his request, de Gaulle met General Dulac, sent from Algiers as an

Many on the left feared that de Gaulle after 1958 would become a tool of the military and they saw his new constitution as the first step to fascism

emissary of Salan. Referring to the recent vote by the Socialists, de Gaulle said: *they don't want de Gaulle. What will you do?* He listened to the details of 'Resurrection' and made some practical criticisms. His last words to Dulac were: *tell Salan that what he has done and what he will do, is for the good of France.* Between 27 and 30 May, telegrams flew across the Mediterranean ordering and then countermanding the operation, supposedly on de Gaulle's authority. The climax came on the morning of 29 May (after de Gaulle's unsuccessful meeting with the Speakers Le Troquer and Monnerville), when Salan received a telegram from Guichard telling him: 'things are going badly. It's for you to play now'. This was, it seems, the go-ahead for Operation Resurrection, confirmed a few hours later by another of de Gaulle's close advisers Pierre Lefranc.[49] But Coty's intervention a few hours after that caused the message to be countermanded at the last moment.

Most of the participants in these events contradict each other on significant details. Lefranc denies that he ever gave Salan any kind of green light, but various other sources are categorical that he did. What about Dulac's visit to de Gaulle? Did de Gaulle tell him, *it would have been immensely preferable* to return to power legally, as Dulac reports or, as Salan records Dulac as reporting, *it is immensely preferable*.[50] Some authors play down the encouragement given to Dulac by pointing out that Pflimlin had just resigned, increasing the chances of a legal solution; others, emphasizing the recent Socialist vote, stress the difficulties of the legal path.[51] De Gaulle's deliberate ambiguity complicates any attempt at interpretation: three times he told Dulac *we must save the outfit [baraque]*. (What outfit: the State? the Republic? the Army? Algeria? France?) And his message to Salan – via Dulac – was not equivalent to a go-ahead for 'Resurrection'. But it remains likely that de Gaulle would, as a last resort, have accepted 'Resurrection' – could he have stopped it? A letter from de Gaulle to his son, written on 29 May after the unsuccessful meeting with Monnerville and Le Troquer, suggests as much: *according to my information an operation is imminent from the south. It is infinitely likely that nothing more will be achieved within a regime no longer capable of deciding anything.*[52]

The best description of de Gaulle's attitude is perhaps that provided by Guichard to a military envoy on 28 May: 'the General firmly intends to pursue matters to the end, and in the eventuality of illegal actions he will take the situation as it comes . . . There must be no let-up in the present pressure nor in the measures taken to favour his legal accession to power.'[53] At the least, having decided to use a military threat – which he had not discouraged – as a means of pressuring parliament to legalize his return to power, de Gaulle ran the risk of setting off a military coup or a civil war. As he had shown in 1940, de Gaulle was a gambler. If the gamble paid off in 1958, it was largely because he was able to become the focus of all hopes. After three years of silence, and having put the RPF behind him, de Gaulle was once again, as he told the press conference, an *homme seul* [man alone]: *belonging to no one, belonging to everyone.*

ALGERIA: 1958–1962

In 1958, as in 1944, de Gaulle's priority was to restore the authority of the state against the forces which had helped him to power: in 1944 the Resistance, in 1958 the Algerian rebels. Visiting Algeria in June he told the Committees of Public Safety which had sprung up after 13 May: *You will not continue to make a revolution.* In July the army was instructed to cease involvement with the committees. At the end of the year, Salan, who had since 13 May combined civil and military power in Algeria, was replaced as military commander by General Challe, and civil authority was entrusted to the economist Paul Delouvrier. This was the first stage of returning the army to its proper role as an instrument of political authority.

For de Gaulle in 1958, restoring the authority of the state primarily required a new constitution. The politicians had accepted de Gaulle's return so that he could deal with Algeria: having done this he would be expendable. For de Gaulle Algeria represented the opportunity to implement his constitutional ideas: Algeria was the means not the end. The summer of 1958 saw the drafting of a new constitution which was massively approved by 80 per cent of voters at a referendum in September. This was clearly a vote for de Gaulle more than a considered approval of a constitution whose exact nature remained to be demonstrated in practice. In December parliamentary elections produced a considerable majority for a newly constituted Gaullist party Union for the New Republic (UNR) and various conservative parties; the left was almost annihilated. This was not necessarily to de Gaulle's liking: he had no more desire to be prisoner of a parliamentary majority than of Algerian putschists. Finally, at the end of the year, de Gaulle was elected President of the new Republic; as premier he appointed his loyal follower Michel Debré. The Fifth Republic had commenced.

These six months were among the most fertile of de Gaulle's career. The variety of reforms effected in such a short space of time brings to mind the early days of Napoleon's consulate. The old man seemed rejuvenated by power. Not only did he transform the constitution of France, but he also embarked upon a major reorientation of France's foreign and financial policies (see the next two sections). As far as de Gaulle was concerned this was only a beginning, but whatever his grand plans for the future, Algeria remained his major immediate preoccupation. He visited the territory five times before the end of the year. The new constitution had given de Gaulle much greater power than any of his predecessors to impose his own solutions, but even so it was to take him another four years to extricate France from the Algerian imbroglio.

What was remarkable about the May crisis was how little de Gaulle had actually said about Algeria: he had committed himself to no position. Although colonial diehards were later to claim that de Gaulle had duped them, de Gaulle had never been an instinctive imperialist. Most ambitious army officers had traditionally coveted colonial postings, but de Gaulle, in his military career before 1940, had chosen where possible to stay on the French mainland. He was one of those who saw France primarily as a continental power and kept their eyes fixed on the German frontier, on the 'blue line of the Vosges', as people expressed it in the late 19th century. De Gaulle's sense of history prevented him from ever linking France's long-term interests with the empire: when one thinks in terms of 2,000 years, what is the significance of a 150-year-old empire? During his posting to the Levant in 1930 to 1931 de Gaulle had written back to a colleague that the

French had hardly penetrated into the region. His conclusion was: *either we achieve this or we leave the area.*[54]

In the 1940s, it is true, de Gaulle had, for contingent reasons, become an ardent defender of Empire. The history of the Free French was intimately linked to France's overseas possessions. Without Africa de Gaulle would have had no base outside Britain, and most of his quarrels with the British occurred because he believed they had designs on French colonies. De Gaulle did recognize that the war had made necessary some evolution in the imperial status quo, and in January 1944 at an imperial conference at Brazzaville in Equatorial Africa he had outlined a vision of economic and political reform for the empire. But, though couched in typically ambiguous terms, this did not call into question the continuation of French sovereignty. During the late 1940s de Gaulle's obsession with international Communism blocked any further development of his colonial thinking.

In the 1950s, however, de Gaulle's ideas started to change. He was resigned to the loss of Indo-China, and at his last press conference before withdrawing from public life in May 1955, he had spoken of *association* with Algeria – quite different from the integration proposed by *Algérie française* diehards. In private conversations between 1955 and 1958 de Gaulle frequently repeated that Algerian independence was inevitable. One visitor was told: *if we let the Algerians vote, they will vote for independence. Of course there remains, as in the past, the possibility of fixing the elections.*[55] It was not only those with liberal views on Algeria who received such confidences. One partisan of *Algérie française* was alarmed to be told in March 1958 that integration was a chimera because the Muslims were not *Provençals or Languedocians.*[56] Soustelle later quoted a 1956 letter to demonstrate de Gaulle's betrayal of his earlier ideas on Algeria, but even this document, written to a fervent partisan of *Algérie française,* studiously avoids mentioning integration.

Soustelle, like so many others, heard what he wanted to hear. De Gaulle did not set him right.

If it is true that de Gaulle was resigned to independence by 1958, why did it take four years to achieve? In his *Memoirs of Hope* de Gaulle claimed that, having no *predetermined plan*, he was convinced of Algeria's right to *dispose of herself*, even if for political reasons this could not be revealed immediately: *I therefore had to manoeuvre without ever changing course, using each crisis as an opportunity to go further*. The only indisputable fact about this idealized account is that de Gaulle manoeuvred so successfully that it is impossible to know what he intended – if he knew himself. In his sinuous policy, dramatic initiatives suddenly interrupted periods of immobility and deadlock, peppered with remarks of gnomic ambiguity.

De Gaulle was studiedly ambiguous from his first visit to Algiers, four days after taking power. Stretching his arms upwards in a huge V he proclaimed, *I have understood you*. The crowd, composed largely of *pieds noirs*, responded with delirious enthusiasm, overlooking the only concrete proposal in the speech: that Muslims must enjoy electoral equality with Europeans and become *Frenchmen with full rights*. De Gaulle bewitched his audience while announcing a future that ended its privileged status. On no occasion did de Gaulle mention the magic word 'integration', and only once, on 6 June 1958, *'Algérie française'* (not included in his collected speeches). Whether this was a lapse or a sop to his audience, de Gaulle never used the phrase again. In October 1958 he announced: *long live Algeria with France, long live France with Algeria*. Whatever that meant, it was not integration. By February 1960 de Gaulle was telling his son of the need to *finish with the myth of* Algérie française *which only disguises the desire of the* pieds noirs *to maintain their domination over the Muslims*.[57] As for the idea of the total integration of Algeria into France, his objections were resolutely unsentimental. He told the Gaullist

De Gaulle speaking in Algeria 1958

deputy Alain Peyrefitte: *We are after all a white European people, with Greek and Latin culture and Christian religion . . . Have you seen the Muslims with their turbans and jellabas? The Arabs are Arab and the French are French. Do you think that French society could absorb ten million Muslims who will soon be twenty million? My village would no longer be called Colombey-les-Deux-Eglises* [Colombey-two-churches] *but Colombey-les-Deux-Mosquées!* [Colombey-two-mosques][58]

There is nothing to indicate that de Gaulle ever believed in *Algérie française*. But he may have hoped he could avoid full independence. For about two years de Gaulle groped for a third way – a middle road between the most intransigent Europeans and the FLN. In October 1958 he announced, at Constantine in Algeria, a five year investment plan to provide educational and economic openings for the Muslims; Salan was exhorted to ensure genuinely free elections which would allow the emergence of an *Algerian political elite*;[59] and in a press conference (23 October 1958) the FLN were offered a *peace of the brave* if they would lay down their arms and negotiate an honourable end to hostilities. The way de Gaulle himself characterized his policy in this first year was that he wanted an *Algerian personality* to emerge *without fixing in advance what the enterprise itself will mould* (3 October 1958). These hopes were vain. The FLN, which now styled itself the Provisional Government of the Algerian Republic (GPRA), refused to lay down arms.

One solution that de Gaulle may have envisaged for Algeria was in the 'Community' – somewhat on the lines of the United Kingdom's Commonwealth – established by the new constitution. France's colonies were to choose between association with France in a federal community, or full independence. In August 1958 de Gaulle undertook a tour of France's sub-Saharan African possessions to sell them the idea of the Community. Although in 1958 Guinea was the only country to choose independence, by 1960 all the others had done the same. In the event therefore the Community was almost stillborn, but it had helped the transition to total independence for sub-Saharan Africa. In Algeria de Gaulle's refusal to talk to the FLN until it had renounced violence made any such transition impossible.

During the first nine months of 1959 the situation was deadlocked. Interviewed by an Algerian newspaper in April, de Gaulle made some comments mildly reassuring to the Europeans; but at the same time he announced that *papa's Algeria is dead*. After a summer of reflection, de Gaulle made a dramatic television broadcast in October 1959. He announced that Algeria's future lay in *self-determination*. The Algerians would be offered three possibilities in a referendum: *francisisation* (de Gaulle's neologism for integration), *secession* (which he painted in lurid colours) or self-government in association with France. The referendum would occur four years after a return to peace, and again de Gaulle appealed to the FLN to negotiate a ceasefire. Again they refused and the impasse continued. Nonetheless this speech represented a key moment in de Gaulle's policy: he had publicly stated the possibility of independence for the first time – even if he described it as secession and made clear that he favoured the third of the three options.

Even this was too much for the *pieds noirs*. In January 1960 their simmering anger exploded in another rising involving many of the same activists as May 1958 – this time with de Gaulle as enemy not saviour. During the so-called 'week of the barricades' key buildings were occupied by demonstrators with the complicity of army units. Had the army fully backed the action, as in 1958,

French forces guard key points in Algiers 1959-60

de Gaulle might have fallen. But although most of his government was in a state of panic – *I felt everything dissolve around me,* he told his son[60] – de Gaulle remained calm. In a spectacular television broadcast, de Gaulle, resplendent in uniform, appealed for army loyalty. The insurrection fizzled out.

In March de Gaulle visited Algeria to reassure army opinion. This 'tour of the messes' was widely interpreted as a move to a more hardline position: the army was told that it would never again suffer the humiliations it had in Indo-China. But, as always with de Gaulle, things were more complicated. It was on the same trip that he launched a new phrase – *an Algerian Algeria linked to France* – that would later inaugurate a new phase of policy. For the moment, however, the war dragged on remorselessly.

In the summer of 1960 occurred an affair which has much exercised those who see de Gaulle as a Machiavellian figure. French intelligence had discovered that some FLN chiefs were willing to explore the possibility of a ceasefire, despite the opposition of the FLN leadership. Clandestine negotiations took place with a representative of de Gaulle, and on 9 June the dissidents, led by Si Salah, found themselves suddenly transported to Paris for a secret meeting with de Gaulle himself. He told them that he was about to launch another public appeal to the GPRA; if this was unsuccessful he would turn back to the dissidents under Si Salah. In the event de Gaulle's renewed appeal to the GPRA (14 June) for the first time received a positive response. Negotiations opened at Melun between French representatives and the GPRA. These proved abortive but in the meantime Si Salah and many of the other dissidents had been purged by the FLN leadership.

De Gaulle's right-wing critics argued subsequently that he had here missed a chance to end the war on French terms. According to this argument, the dissidence of Si Salah and his associates showed that the French army was finally winning the war, and de Gaulle, by choosing this very moment to renew his appeal to the FLN leadership, made clear that he had already cynically decided to 'betray' French Algeria. But, though the Si Salah episode is certainly mysterious – it was extraordinary of de Gaulle to meet these dissident rebel leaders in person and then curious that he showed no interest in following up the contact – he had not somehow missed an opportunity to avoid Algerian independence: Si Salah was no less committed to this objective than the rest of the FLN.

The Melun negotiations failed to produce a breakthrough. In his press conference of 14 June de Gaulle had appealed more directly to the FLN than ever before. He announced an *end to col-*

onization, and referred repeatedly to the *transformation of Algerian Algeria into a modern and fraternal country in union with France.* In spite of this new tone, the Melun meeting foundered on mutual misunderstanding. The

An anti-OAS riot in Paris

FLN negotiators found themselves treated like spies and the French representatives insisted on a ceasefire before negotiations.

The two sides were paralysed again. Meanwhile de Gaulle was coming under increasing international pressure to find a settlement, and within France anti-war feeling was intensifying. In November 1960 de Gaulle spoke in a broadcast of *the Algerian republic which will exist one day.* Soon afterwards he announced a referendum for January 1961 on the principle of Algerian self-determination: hitherto this referendum was to have followed a ceasefire; now it was to precede it. Before the referendum de Gaulle paid, in December, his final visit to Algeria to be met by violently hostile *pieds noirs* demonstrators, and counter-demonstrations by Muslims waving FLN flags. With great physical bravery he plunged into the crowds on several occasions. The visit finally convinced him that a compromise was impossible: not only was independence inevitable, but it would have to be negotiated with the FLN, which clearly enjoyed mass support. The January referendum was a success for de Gaulle: 75 per cent of those voting in metropolitan France approved his policy. Emboldened, de Gaulle opened secret negotiations with the FLN.

During 1961 the tone of his statements on Algeria changed, preparing people for the inevitable. France, he said, viewed *with a perfectly tranquil heart* the idea of losing Algeria, which cost more than it brought in (11 April 1961). Repeatedly he stressed that French power was no longer necessarily linked to imperialism. These remarks led in April to an army putsch in Algiers led by four generals including Salan and Challe. The situation was potentially more dangerous than barricades week. Debré made a histrionic broadcast calling on people to make for the airports and prevent an invasion from Algeria. Again de Gaulle kept calm: he assumed emergency powers and made a dramatic television performance pouring scorn on the rebels and ordering the army to remain loyal. Listened to on the radio by thousands of soldiers, de Gaulle's broadcast swung the day. The putsch collapsed ignominiously.

It was the culmination of de Gaulle's complex and tortured relationship with the army. His writings before 1940 are suffused by a romantic celebration of the soldier's vocation. *The Edge of the Sword* had been written partly to give the military a sense of its value, to combat *the melancholy of the army* in an age that distrusted militarism; *The Army of the Future* offered France's army a new mission of national regeneration; and *France and her Army* opens with the sentence: *France was forged by the sword.* Yet in practice de Gaulle spent much of his life in opposition to the army: in the 1930s, in 1940 and in 1959 to 1961. He could be extremely contemptuous of generals: *every time that the army interests itself in politics it behaves like an idiot: Boulanger, de la Rocque, Pétain.*[61]

Between de Gaulle's idea of the army and the soldiers he actually encountered lay the same sort of gulf as between France and the French. But that did not diminish his reverence for the military calling. The military must simply know its rightful place subordinate to political authority. De Gaulle returned to this theme frequently. *The Enemy's House Divided* suggested that

Germany's defeat in 1918 was partly the fault of the military – Ludendorff and Hindenburg – arrogating political power to itself; the last chapter of *The Edge of the Sword*, 'Politics and the Soldier', is an analysis of the relationship between army and state, warning the military against impatience with the ways of politics. In 1960, during barricades week, de Gaulle told the army that it would become *an anarchic and derisory collection of military castes* if it put any conditions on its loyalty to the State. (He would have justified his own disobedience in 1940 on the grounds that there was no legitimate state to rebel against. The case of 1958 was more dubious: he returned to power thanks to military dissidence – but he also laid great store on being legally invested by parliament, and once back he sought quickly to bring the army to heel.)

After the ignominious collapse of the army putsch there was no further obstacle to formal negotiations with the FLN, which opened at Evian in May. Two years before, de Gaulle had refused to negotiate before a ceasefire, and rejected the FLN's claim to speak for Algeria. Now he wanted to leave Algeria as quickly as possible. But it was to take another ten months and much bloodshed before this was achieved. The Evian talks foundered in June on two issues: the future status of the Europeans in independent Algeria, and whether the Sahara, where oil had recently been discovered, should be included in the Algerian state. De Gaulle ultimately conceded both points and one wonders whether he could not have saved much time and violence by doing so earlier. The French negotiators were handicapped by de Gaulle's obvious desire in 1961 to be rid of Algeria. In the circumstances, it made sense for the FLN to hold out for their demands.

During the winter of 1961–62 the atmosphere in Algeria, and even France, was close to civil war. The opponents of independence formed a clandestine terrorist organization, the Secret Army Organisation (OAS) Terrorism spread to France. The French left, who felt that he was moving too slowly towards independence, also contested De Gaulle's policy. In October 1961 the police violently repressed a peaceful pro-FLN demonstration in Paris. Scores of Arabs were killed – many were drowned in the Seine –

It has been calculated that there were up to 30 attempts to assassinate de Gaulle. Some of these were very half-baked – such as the plan in 1961 to shoot him with cyanide bullets from a gun disguised as a camera – but two came within a hair's-breadth of success. The first of these was on 8 September 1961 when a bomb exploded on the road near Pont-sur-Seine in the Aube as de Gaulle's car was heading towards Colombey. The second was on 22 August 1962 when de Gaulle's black DS Citroën, passing through the village of Petit-Clamart on the way to Villacoublay airfield, was sprayed with bullets. That de Gaulle and his wife were unharmed

was a miraculous escape, apparently due to their refusal to bend down. De Gaulle was unperturbed, and insisted on continuing with the review of the guard waiting for him at Villacoublay. His wife was no less phlegmatic: her immediate worry was whether the chickens in the car boot were still intact. A few days later de Gaulle commented to Alain Peyrefitte that the attack could not have come at a better time (*ça tombe à pic*), and he profited from the resulting wave of sympathy to launch his controversial constitutional reforms. Those responsible for the attack were later arrested, and their leader, Colonel Jean-Marie Bastien-Thiry, was executed.

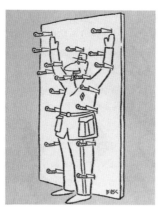

Satirical cartoon coming after the assassination attempts of 1961 and 1962. For de Gaulle, the knives were both real and metaphorical

but this veritable massacre in the heart of Paris aroused remarkably little reaction. During a big left-wing demonstration in Paris on 8 February 1962 eight people died, crushed against the entrance to the Metro during a police charge. Neither of these episodes unduly shocked de Gaulle: in his view it was the duty of the police to keep order.

In the summer of 1961, as a final means of applying pressure on the FLN, de Gaulle floated the idea of partitioning Algeria. When this idea failed he dropped French claims to the Sahara and a settlement was eventually reached in the Evian Accords of March 1962. Although the Accords contained guarantees for the Europeans, they were instantly sabotaged by the OAS, which launched an orgy of violence. Algeria was plunged into chaos and thousands of Europeans streamed into France. In April 1962 a referendum in France approved the Evian Accords by 90 per cent of those who voted. In July 1962 Algeria became independent.

Judged by his original hopes, de Gaulle's Algerian policy was hardly a success. Having held out for a ceasefire before negotiations in 1958, he accepted unconditional talks with the FLN in 1961; having sought a middle way in 1959, he accepted total independence in 1962. His Algerian policy was a long process of retreat. On the other hand, he had succeeded in disengaging France from Algeria without a coup or civil war in France, and had created a large consensus for this policy in metropolitan France. One charge against de Gaulle is that this process need not have taken four years, and that his policy was marked by long periods of inaction – between October 1958 and October 1959, between June and November 1960. But a speedier resolution could have been far worse. Even this gradual pace had sparked two insurrections in Algeria and a wave of OAS terrorism.

Was de Gaulle's policy unduly devious? He might have been able to take more army leaders with him if he had been more open with them. Certainly de Gaulle was always making several moves

AUX ARMES CITOYENS

OAS

The OAS calls on its followers to rise up against de Gaulle

at once: when he was ostensibly reassuring the army during his visit to the messes, he was also launching the notion of 'Algerian Algeria'. He floated almost every conceivable solution – association, independence, partition, provisional partition and repatriation. But rather than cunningly manipulating his opponents, de Gaulle was often feeling his way. As he said in one of his Algerian press conferences, politics is the art of realities. His perception of what these were had to be gradually communicated to the electorate. The phrases in which he draped the stages of his Algerian policy – *the Algerian personality* (1959), *Algerian Algeria* (March 1960) and *the Algerian Republic* (November 1960) – were the instruments of his pedagogy.

However powerful his political position, de Gaulle had to manoeuvre under pressure from many different directions: the army, the settlers, the Algerian rebels, international opinion, increasing anti-war feeling in France and, not least, the reservations of his own supporters. Many Gaullists were fervent advocates of *Algérie française*: including Debré, who was forced to implement a policy he did not approve, and Soustelle, who left de Gaulle's government in February 1960, joined the OAS, and ended up in exile.

Soustelle, Salan and others believed that de Gaulle had cynically betrayed their hopes. But de Gaulle's awareness of realities did not exclude sadness at change. As he put it: *for a man of my generation and background* changes were often *cruel.* Nonetheless there was little sentimentality in de Gaulle's treatment of the *pieds noirs.* De Gaulle the northerner was never captivated by the exuberance of Algerian politics: *they are babblers,* he once said. Possibly also de Gaulle the nationalist was more sensitive to the simple nationalism of the FLN than the tortured double identity – half French, half Algerian – of the *pieds noirs.* It is striking that he paid no tribute and offered no help to the *harkis,* those Muslims who had fought for the French. Ultimately de Gaulle's frustration and near contempt for the *pieds noirs* came from the feeling that Algeria was blocking French policy elsewhere, while he was getting older. He spoke in 1961 of *this affair which absorbs and paralyses us, when we have so many other things to achieve at home and elsewhere.*[62] After the Evian Accords, he solemnly told his cabinet: *Now we must turn towards Europe. For the era of organized continents is succeeding the colonial era.*[63] Or, as he told one of his ministers in January 1963:

Algerian soldiers march during Independence rally July 1962

having given independence to our colonies, we are going to recover our own. Western Europe has become an American protectorate without even realizing it.[64]

DE GAULLE'S FOREIGN POLICY: PURSUIT OF *GRANDEUR*

On 14 January 1963, in the most sensational press conference of his career, de Gaulle announced his veto of British entry to the Common Market and rejected an offer from President Kennedy of Polaris missiles for France as part of a multilateral NATO force. It was no coincidence that de Gaulle made this dramatic gesture so soon after the end of the Algerian War. Now de Gaulle was free to turn his attention to the world stage and unveil his most spectacular foreign policy initiatives. The world should not have been so surprised. Within months of returning to power, he had given notice to his allies that things must change. In September 1958 he presented a memorandum to the British and American governments, requesting that France participate as an equal partner in all political and strategic decisions taken by NATO – which would in effect give France a veto over American nuclear weapons. If this was refused, de Gaulle reserved the right to reconsider France's position within NATO. This opening shot was a warning for the future.

Gaullist foreign policy rested on two basic principles. The first was that the most fundamental reality was the existence of national entities: *people do not die . . . they remain themselves with their own characteristics, their collective temperament, their soul. They live as long as the olive tree.* (At other times the comparison was with the cedar.)[65] Ideologies were only a cloak for national ambitions. This was as true of Roosevelt's liberalism as of Stalin's Communism. The ardent pro-Europeanism of Walter Hallstein, President of the European Commission, disguised a German *ambitious for his country*. In his *War Memoirs* de Gaulle never refers to 'Nazism'; he views the struggle against Hitler simply as a continuation of the

'Thirty Years War' between France and Germany that had begun in 1914. Similarly de Gaulle always referred to 'Russia' not the 'Soviet Union': *Russia will absorb communism like blotting paper absorbs ink.*[66] It follows from this that the relations of states are governed by national interest not ideology: Colonel de Gaulle in 1935 supported a Soviet alliance; and General de Gaulle in 1944 signed one, just as Francis I had allied with the infidel Turk in the 16th century. But alliances, according to de Gaulle, last only as long as

De Gaulle announcing his veto of Britain's application to join the Common Market

the conditions which give rise to them and have no absolute virtue. Foreign affairs cannot include sentiment: *men can have friends but statesmen cannot.* The Atlantic Alliance, signed in 1949 when Europe was weak and under Soviet threat, was not relevant in the same form ten years later.

If the nation state is the only reality, supranationality, for example in the construction of Europe, was a dangerous illusion: an illusion because Europe could only be constructed from existing realities, the nations composing it, and dangerous because a supranational Europe, lacking the collective consciousness that animates a nation, could not command the allegiance which is the precondition of policy. *Policy is action, that is to say a number of decisions that one makes, risks that one runs, all with the support of the people*

(23 July 1964). Who would die for the European Commission? A supranational Europe, with a void at its centre, would be prey to foreign, that is, American, hegemony. NATO was open to the same reproach: the people of Europe would not fight unless they controlled their own defence. Thus France had to be extricated from NATO's integrated command structure; this would actually increase her reliability as an ally. France was ready to be an *integral* part of the Alliance but not an *integrated* one.[67]

The second principle of Gaullist foreign policy was that, in this *difficult* and *dangerous* world (favourite words) of competing national ambitions, France must strive for *greatness* (*grandeur*). After 1958 de Gaulle preferred the word *independence* to describe his aim: freeing France from dependence on others was a prerequisite of *grandeur*. This led to the development of a French nuclear deterrent. Work on a nuclear capability had already started during the Fourth Republic but de Gaulle gave it new priority. France exploded its first atom bomb in 1960 and de Gaulle immediately pushed for the creation of a thermonuclear bomb. He reinforced his case for nuclear independence by arguing that the end of America's nuclear monopoly after the explosion of the first Russian bomb rendered it less likely that America – a late participant in two world wars, he often observed – would risk self-annihilation to protect Europe from Soviet invasion. Self-protection (national interest) would prevail over ideology (defence of the free world): *in their entire history the Americans have never put their national existence in the balance for an engagement abroad. They have never sent more than expeditionary forces which only represented a small proportion of their capacities, even if they fought hard.*[68] More basically, whether the Americans could be relied on or not, de Gaulle felt it to be *intolerable that a great state confide its destiny to the decision and action of another state, however friendly it may be* (11 April 1961).

De Gaulle's fears on this score were aggravated when in the mid-1960s America changed from a doctrine of 'massive retaliation', where any Soviet attack on Europe would be met by a full-scale nuclear attack on the territory of the Soviet Union itself, to one of 'flexible response', where the American counter-attack would be proportionate to the scale of the Soviet attack launched. This made it more likely that the Soviets might risk an attack, and that its consequence might be to turn Europe into the battle-ground of the two superpowers. As for the objection that France's nuclear force was too small to be a credible deterrent, de Gaulle argued that the destructiveness of nuclear weapons was such that even the smallest force had deterrent value: the weak could dis-suade the strong. In reality throughout the 1960s France's nuclear deterrent was too primitive even for this, but it was an index of Gaullist aspirations to independence. In 1963 de Gaulle refused to sign the Nuclear Test-Ban Treaty on the grounds that it merely consolidated the monopoly of nuclear weapons held by Russia, America and Britain.

De Gaulle's policy intentionally disrupted the bipolar interna-tional order which had existed since 1945. De Gaulle assumed that the Cold War would end. For de Gaulle this was both a prophecy and a hope: a prophecy because if the nation-state is the basic reality, power blocs based on ideology – the 'free world' against Communism – are bound to disappear; a hope because France's ability to play a world role would be improved in a multi-polar system. As one commentator put it: the aim was to 'increase [France's] manoeuvrability and to widen her options . . . [to] exploit the structural interstices and the margins of the inter-national system'.[69]

De Gaulle's foreign policy falls into three periods: 1958–62, 1963–7, and 1968–9. Between 1958 and 1962, having presented his terms to the Americans and British, de Gaulle proceeded cau-tiously. He almost certainly expected the memorandum of September 1958 to be refused, as indeed it was: *I asked for the moon*.[70] But he had staked out a position for the future. In 1959

France's Mediterranean fleet was withdrawn from NATO command – a largely symbolic move – and the Americans were forbidden to put nuclear weapons on French soil. For the moment, this was as far as de Gaulle went against the *hegemony disguised as Atlantic solidarity*. He remained inhibited by the Algerian war and by the fact that immediate prospects of reducing cold-war tension were undermined by American-Soviet conflict in Berlin (the Berlin Wall was built in 1961) and in 1962 by the Cuban missile crisis. During these moments of superpower confrontation de Gaulle always advocated the toughest line against the Soviets whereas the British Prime Minister Harold Macmillan and American President Dwight Eisenhower inclined towards conciliation. This is not as paradoxical as it seems: besides demonstrating that his desire for a revision of the Atlantic Alliance did not imply disloyalty to it, de Gaulle feared any compromise between the superpowers at Europe's expense. He remained haunted by his Yalta complex, never missing an opportunity to recall that he had not been at the Yalta conference of 1945, when, de Gaulle believed, Churchill and Roosevelt had betrayed Poland to Stalin.

Since this was hardly the moment for de Gaulle to start distancing himself from America, de Gaulle, thwarted in his desire for France to assert herself on the world stage, decided to turn to Europe. During the Fourth Republic de Gaulle had denounced the Treaty of Rome, which Belgium, France, the Federal Republic of Germany, Italy, Luxembourg and the Netherlands signed in March 1957 to establish the European Economic Community (EEC). Once in power, however, he accepted France's obligations under it but hoped to orient the future development of Europe along very different lines from those envisioned in the treaty. Since 1944 he had nursed the idea that Europe could become a major force, ultimately *the most powerful, prosperous and influential political, economic, cultural and military grouping in the world*. He called in the short term for a *European Europe*, a western-European bloc free of foreign (that is, American) domination, paving the way, in the long term, for a *Europe from the Atlantic to the Urals*. These phrases were characteristically ambiguous, and held out various possibilities: Europe as a second Western force linked to, but not dependent on, America; Europe as a neutral 'third force' mediating between the East and the West; or Europe as a single bloc including European Russia. But whatever de Gaulle's evolving views of Europe's future role, he was consistent in believing that unity must be built on a 'realistic' union of states, not a 'chimerical' fusion of peoples.

De Gaulle was convinced that Europe offered great possibilities to France. As he told one minister in 1962: *Europe is the chance for France to become what she has ceased to be since Waterloo: the first in the world.* The only possible competitors did not count: *Italy is not serious; she doesn't exist. The English console themselves for their decline by saying that they share in American hegemony. Germany has had her backbone broken.* It followed from this that France was, for the moment at least, *the third international reality . . . the only one at the moment, apart from the Americans and Russians, to have an ambition for the nation.*[71]

In 1961 the French presented the 'Fouchet Plan' (named after the Gaullist ambassador Christian Fouchet) for a political union of European states but without any supranational implications. It proposed institutional cooperation between EEC governments on foreign policy and other matters (a possible first stage, de Gaulle later said, to a European confederation). But the Belgian and Dutch governments, who were anyway more favourable to supra-national solutions, were alarmed that the Fouchet Plan omitted any reference to the Atlantic Alliance. Negotiations over the Fouchet Plan became entangled with the issue of British membership of the Community. Having failed to submerge the EEC in a wider free-trade area, the British government had formally applied for entry in 1961. In April 1962 the Dutch and Belgian governments finally vetoed any decision on the Fouchet Plan until British entry. In a press conference (15 May 1962) de Gaulle heaped scorn on the supranationalists – what would Goethe or Dante have achieved writing in Esperanto or Volapuk? he asked – and mocked the supranationalists for desiring the entry of Britain, the country least favourable to supranationalism (hence Macmillan's apt description of de Gaulle's vision of Europe as *'Europe à l'anglaise* [an English style Europe] without the English'). In fact the supranationalists did have a logic: the only condition under which these countries would reluctantly accept a Gaullist Europe was if Britain were present to counterbalance French dominance. This de Gaulle would not allow, and so the Fouchet Plan was buried.

De Gaulle provided cogent reasons for blocking British entry which were shared by many who deplored the brutal style of the French veto: Britain's links with the Commonwealth, her tradition of free trade, and her small agricultural sector would, he argued, fit badly into a protectionist continental bloc with important agricultural interests. His main fear was that Britain would be an American Trojan horse in his 'European Europe'. Macmillan was startled to be reminded by de Gaulle of Churchill's remark about always choosing the open sea before Europe. De Gaulle's view of Britain was reinforced when the Americans cancelled production of the Skybolt missiles ordered by the British government and Macmillan accepted Kennedy's offer to replace them with American-produced Polaris missiles integrated into a multilateral NATO force. Although Macmillan had obtained the same offer for France, de Gaulle, who did not like being offered gifts by others, saw this as definitive proof of British dependence on America.

De Gaulle's unspoken reason for opposing British entry was the fear that it would threaten his vision of a Europe under Franco-German leadership, with Germany as the junior partner.

Having abandoned his ideas for the dismemberment of Germany in the late 1940s, de Gaulle had for a long time argued that the heart of a united Europe must be Franco-German reconciliation, ending the division created by the division of Charlemagne's empire in the ninth century. (It was of course characteristic of de Gaulle to cast the issue in such grand historical terms.) After the failure of the Fouchet Plan, de Gaulle fell back on a narrower version of it and signed a Franco-German Friendship Treaty in January 1963. One of his greatest diplomatic coups had been his courtship of Germany's Chancellor Konrad Adenauer, who had originally been suspicious of him. De Gaulle decided to invite Adenauer to stay at Colombey in September 1958, an honour accorded no other foreign leader. Adenauer was seduced and informally accepted de Gaulle's terms for a special German relationship, including renouncing nuclear weapons (and accepting Germany's post-1945 eastern frontiers, even if the country was reunified). De Gaulle's strong anti-Soviet position over Berlin between 1959 and 1962 consolidated the bond between the two

De Gaulle greeting the German Chancellor Konrad Adenauer at Palais de l'Elysée

men (de Gaulle's policies always had several purposes). In 1962 Adenauer visited France, and the two old men jointly attended mass in Rheims cathedral; two months later de Gaulle paid a spectacularly successful visit to Germany.

But the 1963 treaty was the culmination of this process of *rapprochement* rather than the foundation of still closer friendship. Within Germany many were suspicious of de Gaulle's anti-Americanism, and the Bundestag inserted clauses into the treaty reaffirming German loyalty to NATO; in October Adenauer was replaced by the less accommodating Ludwig Erhard. De Gaulle had underestimated German reliance on American nuclear protection. He had excluded Britain from Europe as an American Trojan horse; but this was even more true of Germany. *Treaties are like young girls and roses,* remarked de Gaulle only six months after signing the treaty, *they last as long as they last*. In public de Gaulle was philosophical about this; in private he was bitter: *the Americans have tried to empty the treaty of any content and make it an empty shell . . . and the German politicians are scared that they are not abasing themselves sufficiently before the Anglo-Saxons! They are behaving like pigs! They would only have themselves to blame if we denounced the treaty and carried out a reversal of alliance by getting together with the Russians.*[72] De Gaulle's foreign policy had reached a dead end. Although he succeeded in pushing the EEC into adopting an agricultural policy favourable to France and blocked attempts to increase the powers of the European Commission (leading in 1965 to a six-month French boycott of Community institutions), from 1963, frustrated in Europe, he moved on to the global stage.

Between 1963 and 1967, when superpower confrontation had died down, there were three strands to de Gaulle's assault on the existing international order: increasing hostility to America, *rapprochement* with Russia and Eastern Europe, and an attempt to extend France's influence in the Third World. In 1964, de Gaulle decided to recognize the Communist government of China. His reasons were cogent: *it is in the interest of the world to talk to them, to trade with them and bring them out from behind their wall of isolation. The politics of the* cordon sanitaire *has never had any result except to make the country that is victim of it more dangerous.* But of course with de Gaulle there was also always the long game to think of: *our kings made an alliance with the Turk against the Holy Roman Empire. They made an alliance with Poland against Germany. I made an alliance with Russia to protect us against Germany. One day I will make an alliance with China to reinforce us against Russia.*[73] And finally de Gaulle would not be unhappy to think that recognizing the Communist government of China would irritate America – which it did.

De Gaulle did his best to irritate America in other ways as well. He missed few opportunities to attack American involvement in Vietnam, the most audacious example being his 1966 visit to Cambodia. Addressing a crowd in the sports stadium of Phnom Penh, he demanded American withdrawal from the region. In 1965 he mounted a campaign against the post-war system that gave the dollar reserve currency status and announced that France was transferring her reserves into gold. Finally, in 1966 France withdrew from NATO, although remaining part of the Atlantic Alliance. All foreign troops were instructed to leave French soil.

As well as attacking America, de Gaulle worked to improve relations with the Soviet Union. As always he had a neat and misty formula to describe his objective: *détente, entente, cooperation.* Starting with a visit to Moscow by de Gaulle's Finance Minister in 1964, an increasing number of exchanges occurred between the two countries. The climax was a visit de Gaulle paid to Russia in June 1966, a few months after leaving NATO. Although the concrete results were limited – France signed trade agreements with Russia and most East European states – the symbolic intent was important. Yet there were contradictions in trying simultaneously to court the Soviet Union and proclaim the end of the cold-war power blocs, thereby anticipating the decline of Soviet dominance in Eastern Europe. Visiting Poland in 1967, de Gaulle announced *you are a great nation*; in reply the Polish leader Gomulka reaffirmed Poland's loyalty to the Soviet Union.

De Gaulle's attempt to improve relations with the Third World was eased by the ending of the Algerian war. The age of colonialism was over; the age of neo-colonialism – or as de Gaulle called it 'cooperation' – had begun. No other country spent a higher proportion of its national income on foreign aid than France. Most of this went to sub-Saharan Africa. Critics denounced the expense of de Gaulle's African policy, but for de Gaulle the gains in influence outweighed the financial costs. African leaders trooped through Paris to pay their respects. French policy towards Africa was run directly from the Elysée Palace, residence of the French President, by de Gaulle's close adviser Jacques Foccart.

At the same time de Gaulle embarked on a global crusade for non-alignment, urging smaller countries to free themselves from dependence on the superpowers. This was the purpose of his tours of Mexico (March 1964), South America (autumn 1964) and Cambodia. France, he claimed, had a historic role to preach liberty to the world. Here de Gaulle shamelessly exploited what he called the *latent moral capital* (9 September 1965) which the Revolution had bequeathed France. While he was in power France sold arms to South Africa, berated the United Nations and in 1964 sent troops to Gabon to prop up the dictatorship of President M'Ba (while denouncing American intervention in Asia). The only country, apart from Ireland, that de Gaulle visited after his retirement was Franco's Spain (to the horror of Malraux). And yet he was also able to declare unblushingly that *there is a pact two thousand years old between the greatness of France and the liberty of the world* (1 March 1941) and that *the nature of France's genius has made her throughout history a crucible and champion of human liberation*

(31 January 1964). These are rather bold claims, and there seems no reason why de Gaulle should have believed France to be exempt from his rule that ideologies are cloaks for national ambition: why should France's universalism have been less suspect than say Roosevelt's liberalism or Walter Hallstein's Europeanism? If de Gaulle was aware of the contradiction, he did not show it – and his rhetoric of non-alignment did have a certain resonance in the Third World.

Even if the practical results of all this activity were limited, there were now few areas of the world where France did not have a distinctive policy. Indeed during 1967 de Gaulle's foreign policy took on a somewhat frenetic air. During the June Six Day War in which Israel defeated her Arab neighbours, de Gaulle, repudiating France's traditional pro-Israeli policy, denounced Israeli aggression (although Israel had reasonable grounds for war) and imposed an arms embargo which hit Israel, a major French customer, disproportionately hard.

In July 1967, visiting Canada, de Gaulle caused a storm by crying *Vive le Québec Libre!* (Long live free Quebec!) This extraordinary gesture of public support for the separatist movement in Canada's French-speaking eastern province scandalized the Canadian government – his hosts – and he was obliged to leave the county prematurely. The irony was that during the war the Anglophone Canadians, may of whom had died to liberate France, had been much more sympathetic to the Free French cause than the French Canadians, who had been among the staunchest Pétainists anywhere.

In December 1967, an article authored by the Chief of the General Staff, but inspired by de Gaulle, announced that France's nuclear forces should ultimately be targeted *tous azimuts* (in all directions), capable of reaching every part of the globe – America as much as Russia. For de Gaulle, in a long historical context, nothing could be taken for granted. As he told

Charles de Gaulle making his three rivers speech urging French Canadians to become their own masters; behind is Premier Daniel Johnson and Mme de Gaulle is sitting passively at the right

De Gaulle's cry of *Vive le Québec libre* was one of the most extraordinary moments in his career, and many people wondered at the time if he had not allowed himself to be carried away in the intoxication of the moment. This is almost certainly not the case. De Gaulle had been following the stirrings of French Canadian nationalism since the early 1960s, and was convinced that Quebec would become independent sooner or later. When invited to attend the celebrations for the centenary of the Canadian Confederation in 1967 he had initially refused on the grounds that Canada had existed much longer than that: *it was founded over four hundred years ago when Jacques Cartier took possession of it for Francis I.* Finally he accepted an invitation from Daniel Johnson, leader, despite his non-French name (*why can't he be called Lafleur like all the others* said de Gaulle) of the Quebec *Union Nationale* party. Before leaving for Canada, Gaulle told an aide: *I won't go to Quebec for tourism. If I go, it will be to make history.*

Peyrefitte already in 1962: *one can never predict where a threat might come from . . . amazing reversals can occur in history. America could explode because of terrorism, or racism . . . and become a threat to peace.*

The Soviet Union could explode because of the collapse of Communism or internal conflicts among her constituent nations. She could become threatening again.[74]

To many, not least his own ministers, de Gaulle's erratic behaviour gave the impression he was losing his grip. One of his former ministers, the conservative politician Valéry Giscard d'Estaing, denounced the 'solitary exercise of power'. But shrewd calculation often lurked behind de Gaulle's most idiosyncratic pronouncements and his most seemingly impulsive actions. His Israeli policy, for example, was based on several factors, including a desire to rebuild relations with the Arab world and a belief that an Israeli victory would embitter her future relations with the Arabs. But the affair also illustrated the limits of de Gaulle's influence. Before the war broke out he had proposed a four-power conference of Britain, France, America and the Soviet Union to resolve the Middle East crisis; only Moscow, supposedly sympathetic to de Gaulle, refused.

In his last year of office (1968–9), de Gaulle's foreign policy entered a third phase characterized by hints of reconciliation with Britain and America. The new American president, Richard Nixon, paid a cordial visit to Paris in February 1969. In the same month de Gaulle had a private dinner with the British ambassador, Christopher Soames, at which he floated the idea of bilateral talks between the two countries. In the event the British government, scenting a trap, revealed de Gaulle's confidential comments to France's European partners: the 'Soames affair' brought Anglo-French relations to a new low.

It is difficult to say whether de Gaulle's feelers to Britain and America heralded a fundamental reorientation of foreign policy because he left office before any change of policy had time to develop. But there were good reasons why he might have contemplated change. The unrest of 1968, discussed below, was followed by a run on the franc that exposed France's economic inferiority to

Germany. De Gaulle may have wanted to counterbalance this by turning to Britain. To the East, the Soviet occupation of Prague in August 1968 proved that the Cold War was not over and dealt a blow to hopes of détente with Russia.

One study of de Gaulle's foreign policy has argued that his change of tack was a sign of success rather than failure and weakness: 'The international system in 1968 and 1969 looked much more like the international system which de Gaulle had hoped to establish in 1958.'[75] Changing American policy in Vietnam and towards China and the beginnings of American détente towards the Soviet Union seemed to vindicate de Gaulle's policies. Despite leaving NATO, the French continued to co-operate closely with it: 'French disruption within NATO turned into cooperation from without the integrated command structure.' De Gaulle had always argued that France's loyalty to the Atlantic Alliance was unquestioned, and would be firmer once she had recovered her independence. Almost his last act as president was to confirm France's membership of the Alliance, which came up for renewal in 1969.

Most people, however, view de Gaulle's foreign policy as a series of failures: the Fouchet Plan was rejected; Germany was not weaned from America; the invasion of Prague and the Soviet attitude during the Six Day War revealed the limitations of rapprochement with Moscow. De Gaulle's achievements were negative: France left NATO; Britain was excluded from Europe; moves towards European supranationalism were blocked. Within Europe de Gaulle underestimated the extent to which France was too strong – and therefore threatening – to be allowed to play the leadership role he coveted, and outside Europe the extent to which she was too weak to do so. The bipolar world remained stubbornly real: the South Americans were no more able to shake off great power tutelage than the Poles simply because crowds turned out to cheer de Gaulle.

But Gaullist policy was more successful than this analysis suggests. De Gaulle often did not want what he said he wanted as much as he wanted to be seen to be asking for it. Even if the Fouchet Plan had been accepted, it would probably only have institutionalized disagreement among European governments. What mattered for de Gaulle was that France was seen to have a policy, to be an active participant in world affairs. De Gaulle's policy should not be judged according to whether it attained some fixed goal. As de Gaulle often repeated: *life is a combat for a nation as for a man* (31 December 1964). The aim was to show that France was participating in the combat. Life was about movement, and *grandeur* was elusive precisely because it was fluid: a *great* nation must pursue a *world policy* (31 December 1963). *For foreign opinion*, de Gaulle later wrote, *our country had suddenly become one of the principal actors in a play where she had previously had no more than a walk-on part.* In reality much of the time France still had no leading role but de Gaulle's lines were interesting enough for this to be sometimes forgotten. French policy was made in France and nowhere else: it was often unpredictable, invariably irritating, sometimes eccentric, frequently sensible – but it was always de Gaulle's.

Gaullist foreign policy also had domestic purposes: de Gaulle saw it as a way of rallying the nation. Here he was only partially successful: there was a danger that people would get bored of the script. Although opinion polls showed de Gaulle's foreign policy to be generally popular, it was decreasingly so. His Israeli policy in 1967 was approved by 30 per cent and opposed by 33 per cent. This had worrying implications for the continuation of the *popular monarchy* by which he had ruled France since 1958.

THE HOME FRONT: 1958–1968
A kind of popular monarchy was how de Gaulle described his regime to his son in 1961.[76] This development had not been

obvious in 1958. The text of de Gaulle's constitution, although reflecting the ideas of his Bayeux speech, was open to interpretation. The powers of parliament were curbed, making it less able to harass the executive: the role of parliament is to legislate, the role of the government is to govern, said de Gaulle. But who would gain from parliament's loss of power: the president or the prime minister he appointed? Certainly the constitution greatly enhanced the role of the president. Not only was he elected by a wider franchise than previously (an electoral college of 80,000 leading political figures) but he was authorized to dissolve parliament, to appeal directly to the people through referenda and to assume extensive special powers in case of national emergency (Article 16). On the other hand, the government, which remained responsible to parliament, was described as 'determining and conducting policy'. This implied an essentially parliamentary system as was the intention of the constitution's main architect, Michel Debré, who had been influenced by the British model.

De Gaulle would never have contented himself with being a figurehead – *Who ever believed that General de Gaulle ought to content himself with opening chrysanthemum shows?* – but the political circumstances shaped the regime in its formative years. For four years de Gaulle was viewed as the only person able to resolve the Algerian problem, and his indispensability enhanced the office he occupied. The Algerian crisis enabled him to deploy the panoply of powers with which the constitution invested him: he held two referenda and after the generals' putsch he invoked Article 16. The government executed policy but de Gaulle conceived it. Nothing illustrates this better than the way in which Prime Minister Debré, who believed in *Algérie française,* was forced to implement a policy which he did not favour: de Gaulle's first reference to the Algerian Republic was slipped into a speech without even informing his startled prémier. 'Does M. Debré exist?'

asked one political commentator in 1959; Fidel Castrato was how others dubbed him.

De Gaulle's style of government did not only affect the prime minister. Other ministers would read about new policies in the newspapers and cabinet meetings were gloomy occasions where ministers could speak on matters affecting their departments but not on general policy. No smoking or side conversations were permitted. As a minister remarked, the meetings were 'funeral wakes with one difference: the corpse speaks.' When Antoine Pinay, Minister of Finance in 1960, ventured to discuss NATO he was rebuked: *Since when does the Finance Minister interest himself in foreign policy?* He left the government soon afterwards. Although occasionally de Gaulle would ask his ministers' opinion on a major policy issue – for example in August 1959 just before the speech on Algerian self-determination – there was no real debate. De Gaulle's Elysée staff became as important as the government itself.

Loyal Gaullists justified this accretion of power by inventing the idea of the 'reserved domain' of issues – Algeria, defence, foreign policy – which were the prerogative of the president. While this was a fair description of reality, nothing in the constitution justified it, and the question was what would occur once the Algerian war was over. After the Evian Accords in 1962 Debré favoured a dissolution of parliament on the grounds that a new parliament should be elected to tackle new problems. This derived from a parliamentary reading of the constitution. Instead de Gaulle replaced Debré, although he had not been defeated in parliament, with the banker Georges Pompidou, one of his former advisers, who had never sat in an elective assembly. Cartoonists depicted him as a valet, always carrying a feather duster. Pompidou's government only narrowly got a majority in parliament. De Gaulle was heading for a showdown with the politicians who had progressively become alienated from him since 1958: conservatives by his Algerian policy, Socialists by his economic policy, liberals by his anti-Americanism, and the Catholic centrists by his disparagement of European unity.

De Gaulle chose to go on the offensive over constitutional reform, proposing that the president should be elected by universal suffrage. He had long nursed this idea. What galvanized him into action was the popular sympathy caused by an OAS assassination attempt in August 1962 which came very close to success. De Gaulle's proposed reform was aimed at consolidating the authority of the president: de Gaulle's successors might not have his historic stature but they would enjoy the legitimacy resulting from popular election. De Gaulle could have chosen no greater affront to France's republican tradition: the last president to be elected by universal suffrage had been Louis Napoleon in 1848, and he had proceeded to abolish the Republic. Ever since then Republicans feared the potential for demagoguery of directly elected heads of state.

As a further provocation, de Gaulle decided to submit the issue directly to a referendum, despite the fact that jurists unanimously agreed that his own constitution required constitutional reform to be submitted to parliament first. There was a political outcry, and Pompidou's government was defeated in a vote of censure. De Gaulle dissolved parliament and announced parrliamentary elections to follow the constitutional referendum. Almost the entire political class, except the Gaullists, opposed the referendum. De Gaulle was accused of violating his own constitution; Monnerville denounced a 'criminal dereliction of duty'. De Gaulle turned the referendum into a test of faith in himself, threatening to resign if he was defeated. In the event 62 per cent of voters approved his reform (46 per cent of the total electorate); this was not a landslide but it was enough. The electorate had ratified his popular monarchy.

Later, at a press conference (31 January 1964), de Gaulle gave his most presidential exegesis of the constitution, denying that there was a *dyarchy* in the Fifth Republic: the president was entrusted, he said, with the *indivisible authority of the state* while the prime minister supervised the day-to-day running of affairs. In the early days Pompidou was indeed even more subordinate than his predecessor. The 'reserved domain' swelled as de Gaulle intervened on matters he would previously have left to Debré. This questionable reading of the constitution ignored one fact: the government remained responsible to parliament, and could only function as an executant of presidential policy as long as it had a parliamentary majority (which was not guaranteed, since parliamentary elections occurred, unless there was a dissolution, every five years, and presidential ones every seven).

De Gaulle's power therefore derived from the parliamentary predominance of the Gaullist party, something he had neither predicted nor wholly desired, hoping to be a president above party. The electoral system chosen by de Gaulle for the election of 1958 (single member constituencies and two ballots) had been intended to prevent the victory of any one party which might tie him down. Although de Gaulle was not directly involved, a few Gaullists rapidly cobbled together the new UNR out of the debris of the RPF. To general surprise the party did well: the Socialist left was crushed and the Gaullists had a majority in combination with the conservatives. At the 1962 elections de Gaulle intervened to appeal for a result which would buttress the success of the referendum: having stood aloof from parties, he was now asking the people to vote for one. This time the other conservative parties were nearly eliminated, and the Gaullists polled more votes than any party in French history (31.9 per cent of the first ballot vote), putting them within 15 seats of an overall parliamentary majority. They achieved a working majority thanks to the support of a small band of sympathetic centrists (Giscard d'Estaing's Independent Republicans).

Even if de Gaulle's power after 1962 rested in practice on the support of a party, he saw his legitimacy as deriving from his own direct contact with the people. Although he did not call another referendum between 1962 and 1968, he evolved a distinctive ritual of government. Like all monarchs de Gaulle showed himself regularly to his subjects: in 'crowd baths' during his regular tours of the provinces, when he plunged into a sea of enthusiastic admirers, to touch and be touched by the 'people'; in frequent television addresses; and in twice-yearly gatherings incongruously described as press conferences. At these occasions, held in the splendour of the Elysée Palace, de Gaulle would deliver a 90-minute prepared lecture without notes – despite his age de Gaulle's memory remained awesome – to the assembled press corps with little pretence of answering the few planted questions. His ministers were all assembled below the podium like obedient schoolboys.

De Gaulle had always been a consummate performer. Having entered history through a radio broadcast, he became in the 1960s an accomplished television performer. The Fifth Republic was born out of a press conference; the Algerian putsch of 1961 collapsed as army conscripts huddled around their transistors to hear de Gaulle. Although de Gaulle's rhetorical skills are difficult to convey in English, some indication of them must be given since they formed such a vital part of his armoury. His repertoire of effects was considerable. He was a master of calculated ambiguity (*I have understood you*) or of simple didacticism: one 1960 television speech on the modernization of the economy opened, *Once upon a time there was an old country encased in tradition and caution* (14 June 1960); another began *Man 'limited in his nature' is 'infinite in his desires'* (31 May 1960). One of de Gaulle's most effective performances was his speech after the Algiers putsch in 1961. He moved from withering contempt for this *foursome of retired generals* to grandiloquent melancholy: *here is the state flouted, the nation*

Satirical cartoon showing de Gaulle conquering the microphones. As president he controlled and commanded the media with ease

defied, our strength weakened . . . By whom? Alas! Alas! by men whose duty, honour and raison d'être *it is to serve and obey*; and from peremptory authority – *I forbid any Frenchman, and above all any soldier, to execute any of their order* – to a final pathetic appeal: *Women of France! Men of France! Help me!* (*'Francaises! Français! Aidez-moi!'*) In the speech during barricades week he had ended by addressing France herself: *Well, my old and dear country, here we are together again, in the face of a testing ordeal*. De Gaulle's language was often stately and pompous – full of the triple cadences which distinguish French rhetoric (as in *duty, honour and* raison d'être above) – but it would suddenly be illuminated by untranslatable flashes of wit or sarcasm, surprising colloquialisms or perplexing anachronisms: the listener was never bored for long. With de Gaulle, the word was all.

Through his style of charismatic leadership de Gaulle was able to reach out to a much wider audience than traditional conservative politicians. This had not been true in the Fourth Republic when the RPF was the refuge of a frightened bourgeoisie. In the Fifth Republic this situation changed. At the elections of 1958 the Communist Party lost 1.6 million votes (30 per cent of its former support), a loss which it never fully recovered in subsequent elections. At least 1 million of these votes went to the Gaullists. Later, at the 1965 presidential election, de Gaulle would win the votes of some 3.5 million former supporters of the left. Malraux had once said that, by breaching the traditional divide between left and right, Gaullism aspired to be the 'metro crowd at rush hour'. Up to a point it succeeded but the breadth of Gaullism should not be exaggerated: the bastions of Gaullist support were in the west and east, traditionally conservative areas; and the Gaullists did much better than the left among women, Catholics and the old. De Gaulle himself, however, scored somewhat better among the workers, and somewhat less well among peasants and the liberal professions than did the Gaullist party. Gaullism may have become France's first successful conservative party, but de Gaulle's own personal appeal stretched further.

De Gaulle ruled France by words – but the performance was a monologue. With parliament's influence so reduced, political discussion revolved around exegesis of de Gaulle's utterances. Opposition leaders, even ministers, were largely absent from the state-controlled television screen. The television news had been known to announce, if de Gaulle were abroad, 'in the absence of General de Gaulle there is no political news today'. Even so de Gaulle often complained to his Minister of Information, Alain Peyrefitte, that French television had fallen into the hands of dangerous reds. When Peyrefitte tentatively suggested that France might adopt a more liberal policy towards broadcasting, on the lines of Great Britain, rather than continue practices more reminiscent of the Soviet bloc or Franco's Spain, de Gaulle would have none of it. This might work for the disciplined British but not the quarrelsome French.[77]

One consequence of the lack of serious opposition to de Gaulle was a tendency towards illiberalism. Fighting OAS terrorism led to the development of parallel police forces whose activities could escape the control of the government. One example of what this could lead to came in 1965 when Ben Barka, a Moroccan political refugee living in Paris, was kidnapped, handed over to Moroccan intelligence and murdered. Although the complicity of French intelligence officers was certain, it was not known how senior the conspiracy went. Such scandals were not new in France, but the style of de Gaulle's rule was conducive to them.

De Gaulle's triumphant homilies to the nation soared above such sordid episodes. His purpose in them was to show that all had changed since his return to power: France, having turned her back on the Fourth Republic, was set on a course of greatness, prosperity and stability. A recurrent theme of his speeches was the need to modernize the French economy, to compensate for imperial decline by becoming a major industrial power. De Gaulle always denied having used the phrase often attributed to him – *let the supply column look after itself* – which implied that he neglected economic issues. Certainly he did not interfere in routine economic management, but he did intervene on matters he considered important. There were two striking examples of this. The first was the Rueff-Pinay plan of December 1958, named after the economist Jacques Rueff who inspired it and Antoine Pinay, the Finance Minister, who reluctantly implemented it. The objective was to break the spiral of inflation which had plagued the Fourth Republic. Public expenditure was to be cut and the franc devalued to make exports competitive. In addition two noughts were knocked off the paper value of the franc which, like the lira, in recent years had been rendered so worthless by inflation that no one took it seriously as a currency: now 100 old francs were to be worth one new one. Finally, restrictions on foreign trade were lifted – the first steps towards removing the protective tariff wall behind which the French economy had existed since the 19th century. Although the plan was remarkably successful, by 1963 there were signs of returning inflation (partly caused by the expense of accommodating the influx of *pieds noirs*) and de Gaulle again intervened to push his sceptical Finance Minister, now Giscard d'Estaing, into announcing a financial stabilization plan (September 1963).

Although the stabilization plan caused a sharp downturn in economic activity between 1964 and 1966, overall de Gaulle's presidency saw impressive economic expansion in France. Yet the economy remained the Achilles heel of de Gaulle's popularity. Economic growth had its victims as well as its beneficiaries: there were violent peasant demonstrations in 1960 and 1961, and a major miners' strike in 1963. The government handled the situation badly, trying to requisition the strikers to continue working. It had to climb down, and de Gaulle's popularity fell to its lowest point: March 1963 was the only time in opinion polls when those 'dissatisfied' (42 per cent) with de Gaulle exceeded those 'satisfied' (40 per cent). Apart from 1963, de Gaulle's popularity never sank below 50 per cent and often went much higher. But when people were consulted specifically about economic issues, between 1964 and 1969 the discontented always outnumbered the satisfied: de Gaulle reached a peak of unpopularity on this issue in February 1969 when 59 per cent were dissatisfied against 19 per cent content. De Gaulle seemed better at persuading the French that France had become a major force in the world, which was arguable, than that most French people were becoming better off, which was indisputable.

The 'dissatisfied' had an opportunity to express themselves in 1965 when de Gaulle's presidential term ended and for the first time the president was to be elected by universal suffrage. De Gaulle delayed announcing his candidature until the last moment but the question had hardly been in doubt. He cast the contest in terms of 'me or chaos': without him, he claimed, *the Republic would quickly collapse and France* [would] *again suffer – but this time without any possible recourse* [that is, to de Gaulle] *– a confusion in the state even more disastrous than previously* (4 November 1965). It was a singularly illogical stance for someone who claimed that his main achievement had been to provide France with stable institutions. De Gaulle, feeling confident of the result and considering it undignified to fight an election campaign, refrained from using the television time allowed to candidates – and suffered instead the indignity of failing to win a majority at the first round: he obtained 43.7 per cent of the vote, while his two main rivals François Mitterrand and Jean Lecanuet obtained 32.2 and 15.8 per cent respectively. The result partly reflected the sheer novelty of seeing opposition figures on a screen usually monopolized by de Gaulle: the relative youth of Mitterrand (49) and Lecanuet (45) made a refreshing contrast with the ageing monarch of the Elysée. It was, wrote one journalist, as if the television station had 'fallen into the hands of daring rebels'.[78] Before the second round, de Gaulle performed effectively on television, while Mitterrand's last appearance was briefly affected by a 'technical hitch' which made him sound like Donald Duck. At the second ballot, De Gaulle scored 54.5 to

Mitterrand's 45.5 per cent – but the fact of having been forced into a runoff at all had shown that even he was vulnerable. The spell was broken.

Although the election had been a blow to de Gaulle's prestige, it had paradoxically helped to legitimize the institutions he had created. After all, Mitterrand could no longer denounce the Fifth Republic and the idea of a directly elected presidency, once he had himself stood for election as president of that Republic. On the other hand, now that de Gaulle's constitution was less contested, he could not so convincingly argue that he was the only guaran-

François Mitterrand's opposition to de Gaulle had a long history. The two men had first met in 1943 when Mitterrand, leader of a Resistance movement of former POWs, was hoping that de Gaulle would support his leadership over that of his rivals. The meeting was frosty, possibly because de Gaulle suspected, with reason, that Mitterrand, who had for two years supported the Vichy regime, had been more sympathetic to the conservative Giraud than to him. In 1944, when de Gaulle returned to Paris, he found the 27-year-old Mitterrand installed as the Secretary General for Prisoners of War in the provisional government formed by the Resistance to await his arrival. *You again* were de Gaulle's alleged words on seeing Mitterrand, and he did not keep him in his government. Mitterrand soon became a pillar of the Fourth Republic which de Gaulle so despised. In 1958 he was one of the most vociferous opponents of de Gaulle's return to power. He declared: 'in 1944 General de Gaulle's two companions were Honour and Nation. His companions today are . . . Coup and Sedition.' For several years after 1958, Mitterrand was in the political wilderness, and in 1964 he wrote a book attacking the Fifth Republic as a 'permanent coup d'état'. The irony was that in 1965, Mitterrand, standing to defend the colours of the left, also found himself winning the votes of all the right-wing enemies – from nostalgic Pétainists to former supporters of *Algérie française* – whom de Gaulle had accumulated over the last 20 years. The only consistency in Mitterrand's sinuous career was opposition to Gaullism.

tor of political stability in France – 'me or chaos'. At the 1967 parliamentary elections he nonetheless used the tactic again, intervening in the election campaign to ask for a parliamentary majority which would allow him to govern effectively: more explicitly than ever he was assuming the role of a party leader. But on this occasion the Gaullists obtained only the narrowest of majorities. The government responded by asking parliament to grant it economic decree powers for a limited period.

De Gaulle was not wholly insensitive to the

Francois Mitterand, lifelong opponent of Gaullism, at the Grand Quevilly

growing signs of opposition. After 1965 he revived his idea for an *association of capital and labour* – or labour *participation* as he now preferred to call it. Although de Gaulle harped on this theme frequently, nothing more was achieved than a minor profit-sharing scheme in 1967. Pompidou was sceptical about the whole notion of *participation* and de Gaulle failed to make him act decisively. No doubt this was partly because de Gaulle himself was unsure how to translate his vague notion into practice, but it also reflected the increasing influence of Pompidou, who had begun to acquire a political stature of his own.

De Gaulle had resuscitated his old idea of participation partly because he realized that his hold over the French people was weakening, but neither he nor anyone else predicted the storm that lay ahead. At the end of 1967 he greeted the new year *with serenity*. A famous article in *Le Monde* in March 1968 was entitled 'La France s'ennuie' (France is bored). Seven years of Gaullist rule had become stifling. Even de Gaulle was bored. In April he told an aide: *this no longer amuses me much; there is no longer anything difficult or heroic to do.*[79] He need not have worried: within three weeks his regime was on the verge of collapse.

1968 AND AFTER

1968 was a year of protest throughout the world. What made France different was that student demonstrations in early May were joined, after two weeks, by massive strikes which so severely paralysed French life that by the end of the month de Gaulle's survival seemed in the balance. A student revolt (3–13 May) became a social crisis (13–27 May) which developed into a political crisis (27–30 May).

The start of street demonstrations in Boulevard Saint-Michel, Paris. Several hundred students and police received hospital treatment after numerous battles between police and students

There were many reasons for this escalation: an education system unable to absorb a massive expansion in student numbers; social discontent resulting from the economic stabilization plan; and a political system which had so weakened intermediary institutions between president and people as to stifle outlets of protest. Most of all, the events of 1968 were also a profound politico-cultural upheaval, a carnival of protest against a stultifyingly authoritarian political system. Students occupied the Odéon theatre and constructed endless verbal utopias; the workers of the Berliet truck factory rearranged the sign over their factory to read *Liberté*. Wordplay was integral to 1968. Having for ten years ruled France with words and reduced his opponents to silence, de Gaulle, confronted by a revolution of graffiti, slogans, tracts, speeches, and manifestos, was reduced to impotent silence in the Elysée. Having turned politics into theatre, de Gaulle now confronted a movement which turned theatre into politics. He described the situation as *insaissisable*, impossible to get a hold on. Army putschists who defied the state could be summoned to obedience; now the state itself seemed to be slipping through his fingers like sand.

There was a fundamental cultural abyss between the student protestors, who celebrated individualism, self-expression, and personal freedom, and de Gaulle's austere patriotism, in which the highest value was the sacrifice and sublimation of individualism in the nation. There had already been straws in the wind in the previous year. In 1967, de Gaulle had agreed to the legalization of contraception, under pressure from Pompidou and other ministers. But he admitted that he had never taken a decision which went so *against the grain* (*à contre coeur*) and he drew the line at the State paying the cost of contraceptives: *the French want greater moral freedom. But we're not going to start reimbursing sex! One might as well reimburse people for buying cars.*[80]

De Gaulle's first reaction in May 1968 was that no one could take *these kids and jokers* (*ces gamins, ces rigolos*) very seriously. In the second week of May, as the joke seemed to be going on too long, de Gaulle urged his ministers to instruct the police to give no quarter in repressing the protests. At one point he contemplated sending in the army. If de Gaulle had been listened to, it is likely that the events of May, in which miraculously no one died, would have degenerated into a bloodbath. On 24 May de Gaulle addressed the nation saying that the crisis demonstrated the need for a 'mutation in society' and announcing a referendum on participation. The broadcast was a fiasco: de Gaulle seemed old and tired, his remedies vague. Often he had turned a situation around through a speech; this time he only made things worse. Up to then the student demonstrations had mostly been confined to the Latin Quarter on the Left Bank, but now many students surged across the river to the Right Bank, and some of them even tried to burn down the Stock Exchange.

While de Gaulle floundered, Pompidou rose to the occasion with inexhaustible energy, attempting a conciliatory policy towards the protestors in the hope of channelling the revolt into concrete demands which could be met through negotiation. He conducted frantic talks with trade-union leaders. Meanwhile de Gaulle prowled helplessly around a largely deserted Elysée. On 28 May his close adviser Jacques Foccart found him in despair: *what can I do? Is there anything that can be done . . . The French people is letting itself die . . . They followed me – or a tiny minority did – in 1940. They followed me in 1958, with a lot of reservations. But the enemies reappear and destroy everything. This is a country which is disintegrating and I can do nothing about it. How can one stop a country disintegrating if that is what its people want to do?*[81]

On 27 May Pompidou's negotiations resulted in an agreement with the trade unions, but the agreement was rejected almost immediately by rank-and-file workers. Scenting blood, the politicians moved in: on 28 May Mitterrand declared himself ready to form a provisional government; the Communist Party called a massive demonstration for 29 May. Now de Gaulle acted. On the morning of 29 May, he informed Pompidou that he was postponing that day's cabinet meeting because he was tired and wanted to go to Colombey: *I am old. You are young*, he told Pompidou on the phone. *It is you who are the future . . . But I tell you, I will be coming*

Trade unionists and students demonstrating against de Gaulle in May 1968, 'La Chien Lit' [havoc] refers to de Gaulle's much quoted remark 'Yes to reforms, no to havoc'. The anachronistic word 'chienlit' initially caused much perplexity

back. I embrace you. This was disconcerting enough, but a few hours later Pompidou was alarmed to hear that de Gaulle had completely disappeared.

In fact, in almost total secrecy, de Gaulle had flown by helicopter, accompanied by his wife, to Baden-Baden, the site of French forces in Germany under the command of General Massu, one of the generals who had helped de Gaulle back to power in 1958, although he had not fully approved of de Gaulle's subsequent Algerian policy. De Gaulle greeted Massu with the words *C'est foutu* (It's all over). But after 90 minutes in Germany, de Gaulle, who had been joined by his son, returned to Colombey having made his resolutions. That evening de Gaulle's spirits seemed to have recovered. Reciting a few lines of poetry to his aide François Flohic, he asked him to guess who had written them, and then revealed himself as their author. On the next day he broadcast again (on the radio only). This time the tone was tougher than six days before: he denounced the threat of Communist dictatorship and demanded a return to order; the referendum announced on 24 May was postponed and instead parliament was dissolved and elections announced. An hour after this speech, the streets of Paris began to fill up for a massive Gaullist demonstration on the Champs Elysées. This event had been planned for several days but its size – possibly one million demonstrators – surpassed expectations. The 'events' of May were over.

De Gaulle's secret helicopter journey to Baden-Baden on 29 May 1968 was one of the most puzzling events of that month

29 May 1968 was one of the most dramatic days of de Gaulle's career. Was it a new flight to Varennes, another 18 June, an appeal to the army, a desperate retreat? There are two interpretations of de Gaulle's secret journey to Germany. One, believed by Massu and Pompidou, is that, entirely demoralized, he had decided to give up, and was only revived by Massu's encouragement: *It was providence that placed your husband in my path on May 29*, de Gaulle later told Mme Massu. The other view is that de Gaulle had executed a brilliant tactical manoeuvre, creating momentary panic in France and then returning to restore the situation.

The evidence is inconclusive. De Gaulle arrived in Germany with enough luggage to make it plausible that he intended to remain, and twice during his short visit he asked the German government to be informed that he was staying (his order was not carried out). However, de Gaulle had originally intended to meet Massu in eastern France and only ended up going to Germany because he had failed to make radio contact with him. It is possible that de Gaulle had set off with a firm purpose – to assure himself of the loyalty of the army – and then given way to momentary despair; equally it was not unknown for him to play the role of the gloomy pessimist to obtain the encouragement he required. The volatility of de Gaulle's mood at this stage makes it quite credible that, fluctuating between resolution and despair, he had, as he himself later put it, considered *every possibility without exception*. The only certainty is that, whatever his ultimate aim, he had, as so often, aimed to produce the maximum surprise. It is also true that his timing had been impeccable. The politicization of the May events – Mitterrand's statement and the Communist demonstration – had made the situation less *insaissisable*: at last there was a clear opponent. And although de Gaulle knew as well as anyone that the last thing the Communists wanted was a revolution that could have got out of hand, he was now able to play the anti-Communist card.

The legislative elections of June 1968 therefore took place on the theme of a return to order. They resulted in a Gaullist landslide: for the first time ever one party obtained an overall majority. Nonetheless de Gaulle's last 11 months in power were unhappy ones. In foreign policy there was a retreat; and on the economic front, a devaluation of the franc, badly hit by the events of May, was only narrowly averted in November. As for the lessons of May 1968, there was a difference of view between the new parliament, which was highly conservative, and de Gaulle, who saw a confirmation of his diagnosis that reforms were necessary. When the new education minister, Edgar Faure, proposed a major reform of the education system – with de Gaulle's full support – there were rumblings among the Gaullist deputies.

In February 1969 de Gaulle announced that he was going to submit two reforms to a single referendum: a measure of regional decentralization and a reform of the Senate. Although he presented these as part of his project for increased participation, the reforms were of minor importance (and not really related). Their main purpose was to provide de Gaulle with a pretext to renew the direct 'contract' between himself and the people. He believed rightly that the parliamentary elections had been a reflex of social panic rather than a test of confidence in himself. Although it soon became clear that the referendum would go against him, de Gaulle resisted all possible escape routes, such as a postponement of its date. Originally conceived as a means of restoring legitimacy, the referendum now became an elegant means of leaving power without being forced out (there was no requirement to resign after defeat in a referendum) and without declining into the shipwreck of old age. His prestige would remain intact. He told one visitor: *I will be more for France than if I had left for the banal reason that my period of office had expired.*[82]

Defeat was all the more probable since Pompidou, who had been replaced as premier in June 1968 by Maurice Couve de

Murville, de Gaulle's former foreign minister, made it clear that if de Gaulle left power he would be a candidate for the succession. Pompidou, who had started entirely in de Gaulle's shadow, had emerged as a powerful figure in his own right. He had at first been startled by de Gaulle's seeming paralysis during the events of May – 'De Gaulle no longer exists, he is dead, there is nothing left', he remarked to an aide – and then deeply resentful at having been left in the lurch on 29 May. He felt released from any obligation of personal loyalty to de Gaulle, and his existence as a possible successor undermined de Gaulle's usual argument of 'me or chaos' since Pompidou was the man who had staved off chaos during May. On 27 April, the reforms proposed in the referendum were rejected by 53 to 47 per cent. Immediately de Gaulle issued his last official communiqué: *I am ceasing to exercise my functions as President of the Republic. The decision takes effect at midday today.*

Apart from a formal telegram of congratulation to Pompidou on his election as president, he made no further public statements. De Gaulle had spent the election campaign in rural seclusion on the west coast of Ireland, savouring the windy landscapes. Before returning to France he was entertained to lunch by the Irish President Eamon de Valera. De Gaulle proposed a toast to *L'Irlande unie* (United Ireland); perhaps it was not by chance that at this moment the microphones failed, and few heard him.

Returning to France, de Gaulle

De Gaulle had long felt a certain sentimental affinity for Ireland. On his mother's side de Gaulle descended from the Irish MacCartan clan, while his paternal grandmother, Joséphine (née Maillot), had written a biography of the Irish nationalist Daniel O'Connell entitled *The Liberator of Ireland*, which de Gaulle seems to have much admired. Apart from these family connections there was also the fact that, as de Gaulle told Peyrefitte in 1964: *Ireland is not Anglo-Saxon! The English have treated the Irish more or less like the French of Canada, that is to say like half-men. But Ireland has held out over the course of the centuries in the face of Anglo-Saxon pressure. It has kept its personality.*

retired to Colombey to write a second set of memoirs, *Memoirs of Hope,* chronicling his period in office since 1958. He made no further public statements; never again did he visit Paris, apart from an incognito appearance at the christening of a goddaughter. He contrived to be absent from France on the anniversaries of 18 June so that others could not use his glory for their purposes: in June 1970 he visited Spain, in 1971 he planned to go to China. At Colombey de Gaulle received few visitors. He wrote, read – mainly Shakespeare, Chateaubriand, Sophocles and Claudel, so he told Malraux – and ruminated on human ingratitude and the decline of France. The first volume of the *Memoirs of Hope,* entitled *Renewal (1958–62),* appeared in the bookshops in October 1970 without any advance publicity – a final theatrical effect. Only two

De Gaulle's funeral at Notre Dame

chapters of the second volume, *Endeavour,* were finished when de Gaulle, having sat down after dinner to play a game of patience, died suddenly on 9 November 1970, 13 days before his 80th birthday.

Following his instructions, there was no state funeral. A requiem mass, attended by world leaders, was held in Notre Dame. On the same afternoon de Gaulle was buried at Colombey, after a simple ceremony, attended only by his family, some villagers and 'companions' from the Free French days. The intimacy of the final ceremony was entirely characteristic of a man who had always preserved a sharp separation between his private and his public personality.

Conclusion: The Achievement and the Legacy

De Gaulle's historic stature now seems beyond question, but there is still debate as to where his significance lies. He was a soldier who spent much of his career in opposition to the army, a conservative who embraced change, and a man of overweening ambition who twice renounced power voluntarily. The party that bears de Gaulle's name in France today is on the right, yet in a recent opinion poll asking which Frenchmen were most authentically in the tradition of the French Revolution, de Gaulle emerged first with 30 per cent, followed far behind in second place by the early-20th-century Socialist leader Jean Jaurès with 8 per cent.

In *The Edge of the Sword* de Gaulle observes that history will always remember those individuals who offered their contemporaries elevating ideas of *grandeur* over those who merely provided them with something useful: Napoleon will always stand above Parmentier (an 18th-century French chemist and doctor best known for having given his name to the French version of shepherd's pie – *hachis parmentier*). As far as de Gaulle is concerned, three outstanding achievements guarantee him an enduring place in French history. First, thanks to de Gaulle the Liberation of France in 1944–45 took the form of a relatively smooth transfer of power to a French government enjoying a wide degree of legitimacy both at home and abroad. France was spared both an allied military government (like Italy) and a period of prolonged civil disturbance (like Greece). As a result, France, crushed in 1940, had by 1945 recovered something approaching great-power status: she had a zone of occupation in Germany and a permanent place on the United Nations security council. De Gaulle's methods in achieving these objectives were not necessarily the only ones that could have been pursued. De Gaulle doubtless had the faults of his virtues: his vigilance towards his allies sometimes verged on paranoia. And it is probable that the British and Americans would anyway have wanted to build France up again. But the speed of this process owes much to de Gaulle.

In 1940 de Gaulle had announced that France had lost the battle but not the war. The novelist Antoine de Saint-Exupéry, who was no Pétainist, rejected this formulation: 'tell the truth, General, France has lost the war. But the Allies will win it.' Preferring to go to America rather than join the Free French, he later died in combat in North Africa having to the end opposed de Gaulle's attitude to Giraud: in his view all that mattered was to fight the Germans. Of course Saint-Exupéry was right about the winning of the war, and de Gaulle knew it, but he was wrong not to see that de Gaulle's stance guaranteed the existence of a French state in 1944 to look after French interests. In a real sense de Gaulle had redeemed French honour, and given the French people in 1944 a sense of self-respect. His government then peacefully implemented a major series of social reforms and restored democracy.

De Gaulle's second major achievement was to extricate France from Algeria without a civil war in mainland France or a successful army coup – both of which were eminently possible outcomes. What was also remarkable was the speed with which the French put Algeria behind them in the 1960s. De Gaulle's insistent pedagogy played an important role here. *What have I ever been but someone who wanted to teach,* he once remarked. In speech after speech he lectured the French, as once he had lectured the cadets of St Cyr, putting France's empire in historical perspective, explaining how it had been acquired after 1870 to compensate for France's continental decline and how that era was now over. He offered the French new adventures on other stages. Dean Acheson, secretary of state under President Harry Truman, said of Britain in the 1960s that she had lost an empire but had not yet found a role; de

Gaulle announced France's 'winds of change' – Harold Macmillan's phrase for the necessity of decolonization – but, unlike Macmillan, he succeeded in offering a new vocation to a country whose post-colonial traumas could easily have been much more acute than Britain's. Thanks to de Gaulle the French did not experience the loss of Algeria as the humiliating defeat it was in some respects; they adjusted better than the Americans in the immediate aftermath of Vietnam.

Thirdly, in the constitution of the Fifth Republic, de Gaulle provided France with political institutions that have proved effective for the last 45 years. For the first time since the Revolution France's political institutions are no longer contested by any important political group. This has led one recent historian to describe de Gaulle as France's George Washington.[83] Nation and state have finally been reconciled. Not just politically, but also diplomatically and economically, 1958 is a landmark in French history. The new constitution overhauled France's political institutions; the Atlantic Memorandum prefigured a reorientation of foreign policy; and the Rueff-Pinay plan stangled inflation.

Accepting that 1958 was a watershed in French history does not, however, require us entirely to agree with de Gaulle's reading of that history, in which the Fourth Republic represented 12 lost years of inflation, devaluations, and instability, mercifully superseded by a regime bringing stability, prosperity and prestige. When visiting French cities in the early years of his presidency de Gaulle would affect surprise at the speed of their recovery since the war – as if the Fourth Republic had not existed. It is true that the Fourth Republic had many faults, even if the two features which most weakened it – inflation and colonial problems – were both legacies of de Gaulle's period as head of the Provisional Government: his choice of Pleven over Mendès France, and his decision to hang on to Indo-China. Even so, the Fourth Republic should not be written off. Many of de Gaulle's most striking achievements built upon the work of his reviled predecessors: the foundations of Franco-German reconciliation had been laid by the establishment of the steel and coal community in 1951; the decision to construct an atomic bomb had been taken in 1957; the decolonisation of black Africa, completed by de Gaulle, had been prepared by the important reforms of Gaston Defferre in 1957; the spectacular expansion of the economy had started in the early 1950s. The arrival of de Gaulle to power also enabled France to implement the provisions of the Treaty of Rome, which had been negotiated by his predecessors but were only due to come into effect in 1959. As Raymond Aron remarked: 'the ruse of Reason [Hegel's phrase for the hidden logic of history] was favourable to us. The Gaullists would not have signed the Treaty in the first place; the Fourth Republic would not have been capable of applying it.'[84]

There were, then, continuities between the policies of the two regimes. It is also true that many of the Fourth Republic's leading politicians already accepted that some degree of institutional reform was inevitable. Irrespective of de Gaulle, it is likely that measures would have been taken to strengthen executive power, without necessarily going as far as de Gaulle was to do. If this is true, the transformation of France's political insitutions after 1958 can be seen in part as a consequence of the social and economic changes occurring in France since 1945: only a stronger state had sufficient authority to guarantee social cohesion during such rapid modernization. The Fifth Republic, so the argument goes, was the regime of the technocrats, and Gaullism an instrument of modernization. In this context it is striking that political scientists have demonstrated a strong correlation between Gaullist electoral success and the more economically dynamic areas of France. Having defied history in 1940, de Gaulle's role after 1958 was more to embrace and dramatise it – to give meaning to inevitable change, as he did with decolonization. Franco-

German reconciliation may have started in the 1950s, but it was de Gaulle who publicly embraced Adenauer when the Franco-German Treaty was signed in 1963.

What remains of de Gaulle's legacy in France today? There can be no straightforward answer to this question. In some respects France remains faithful to the principles he established. The French President is the most powerful head of State in any western democracy; France remains outside NATO and French foreign policy often sounds a distinctive note; although it was much contested in de Gaulle's lifetime, few in France now oppose the French nuclear deterrent; French policy in black Africa continues to follow Gaullist lines; France tries to retain privileged relations with Arab states; and for all its ups and downs the Franco-German relationship still remains a guiding principle of French policy and the core of the European Union. Perhaps the greatest testimony to de Gaulle's success was that his life-long enemy François Mitterrand remained so faithful to the Gaullist inheritance when he became President in 1981. It was often remarked that Mitterrand's style was almost more Gaullist than de Gaulle.

But contemporary France has in many ways turned its back on de Gaulle's legacy. The Maastricht Treaty has taken France down a road of European supranational integration on a scale beyond de Gaulle's wildest nightmares. Three periods of cohabitation (1986–1988, 1993–1995, 1997–2002) between the President and a hostile parliamentary majority have substantially weakened the authority of the presidency: between 1997 and 2002 the Gaullist President Jacques Chirac had as little power as de Gaulle's much reviled Fourth Republican predecessor René Coty. Various amendments to the constitution, most notably one reducing the presidential term from seven to five years, have led some commentators to suggest that the Fifth Republic is quietly mutating into something so different that it should be called the Sixth. Most importantly, although Mitterrand would from time to time invoke France's 'rank', de Gaulle's successors have abandoned talk of pursuing a policy of *'grandeur'*. Most people believe that this aspect of Gaullism, so central for de Gaulle himself, has proved itself an unsustainable anachronism.

Many commentators would share the verdict of Lord Gladwyn, a Foreign Office diplomat who had known de Gaulle both during the war and later, as British Ambassador in Paris: 'undoubtedly the General's chief failing – and in the long run it was unfortunate – was to cast his country into a role which was beyond her power.'[85] Were de Gaulle's ambitions for his country delusions of *grandeur* inappropriate for France in the 20th century? Already in 1940 he struck many people as like a relic from another age. One observer remarked upon his 'long ivory-coloured face which might well have rested on a ruff'; another wrote: 'his features made one think of a medieval painting and one imagined him in chain mail and with a helmet.'[86]

But de Gaulle was not really a noble anachronism. Indeed, some critics have argued that, far from being some 20th-century Don Quixote, tilting at impossible windmills of *grandeur*, de Gaulle was really a supreme realist, even a cynical Machiavellian, who believed in nothing. Analysing the causes of Germany's World War One defeat in his first book, de Gaulle contrasted the German leaders' lack of moderation, their contempt, derived from Nietzsche, for the *limits marked out by human experience and good sense*, with the French sense of classical order and proportion: *in a French garden no tree tries to blot out the others with its shadow.*[87] Ten years later in *France and her Army* he praised the *ancien régime* for its empiricism and respect for circumstances: *wary of abstractions but savouring realities, preferring the useful to the sublime, the opportune measures to resounding ones, searching, in each particular problem, for the practical not the ideal solution, with few scruples as to the means, showing greatness, however, in its respect of a just proportion between the ends pursued and the state's capacities.*[88] As much as he celebrated *grandeur*, de Gaulle advocated a sense of proportion. Bismarck he admired for knowing when to stop; Napoleon he criticized for the opposite: his fall was *the just anger of reason, the tragic revenge of moderation [mesure]. The force of circumstances, things being what they are, men being what they are and the world being what it is*: these phrases recur throughout de Gaulle's speeches and writings. Though de Gaulle was far from always prescient, he was remarkably ready to adapt.

Yet de Gaulle was neither Don Quixote nor Machiavelli. His talk of *grandeur* was always flavoured with a strong dose of realism; his realism was elevated above mere opportunism by his belief that France could carve out some kind of world role for herself. To be great, de Gaulle had said in the epigraph to *The Edge of the Sword*, misquoting *Hamlet*, is *to sustain a great quarrel*. When lecturing at St Cyr in 1921 he had warned his audience above all against fatalism; similarly in the 1940s and in the 1960s he exhorted the French to believe in themselves as a great nation: *grandeur* was an attitude rather than a concrete goal. De Gaulle had few illusions about the decline in France's material power. As he famously remarked to Malraux: *my only rival is Tintin! We are the small who refuse to allow ourselves to be cheated by the big. Only, no one notices the similarity because of my size.*[89] (A few years later he might have chosen Asterix as his rival, who had the further advantage of being French not Belgian.) On one occasion de Gaulle described his policy during the war as one of bluff, throwing dust in the Allies' eyes so that they might be blinded into thinking that France was great. This does not mean that *grandeur* was merely posturing: it was a question, as for Tintin, of playing the limited cards one held to greatest effect.

A perfect example of this was the Berlin crisis of 1959. Of all the Western leaders de Gaulle was the firmest in advocating no capitulation to Khrushchev's demands – thereby consolidating his relationship with Adenauer. Yet the brunt of any military showdown – which de Gaulle did not believe likely – would have been borne by America and Britain. De Gaulle's policy was to push the Americans into standing firm. He got the credit from Adenauer for being Germany's most steadfast ally despite his relative military weakness and the fact that it was America and Britain who were running the real risks.

One way *grandeur* could be translated into policy was through the pursuit of *independence*. Although this favourite Gaullist word has been as much criticized as de Gaulle's notion of *grandeur*, it should not be seen as signifying some blinkered refusal of 'interdependence', which de Gaulle saw as inevitable, but rather as a rejection of 'dependence' – not unnatural in someone who had witnessed the fateful dependence of French foreign policy on Britain in the 1930s or experienced such a humiliating dependence on the Allies during the war. It was de Gaulle who in 1940 had announced that *France is not alone*. And in 1959 it was de Gaulle who told the federal assembly of Mali about to receive independence that he preferred the term 'national sovereignty' to independence: *the world being what it is, so small, so narrow, so interlinked, no one enjoys total independence* (12 December 1959).

De Gaulle could perhaps best be described as an 'existential' nationalist as opposed to an 'essentialist' nationalist in the style of, say, de Valera or Franco. While he viewed history as an existential struggle for survival between nation states, he did not fight to preserve a particular essentialist vision of what France should be. Contrary to many French conservatives – and not only conservatives – one would never find de Gaulle celebrating France as, say, the repository of peasant or rural virtues – for all that he was attached to the bleak French plains and forests around Colombey. Where Pétain, born into a peasant family, felt in 1940 that defending France required remaining on French soil among the French people, de Gaulle left for London to defend France as an idea, as the continuity of an historical entity. This does not mean that de Gaulle's France was an abstract concept. His attachment to France was as to a physical being: *one loves one's country like a mother*, he told the soldiers serving under him in 1913; one of his BBC broadcasts in 1940 is a sort of prayer to *Our Lady of France holding out her hands to her 'sons'* (16 December 1940); *nothing is lost for a Frenchman when he rallies to France his mother*, he proclaimed (25 January 1960). But none of this tied his vision of France down in any precise way.

De Gaulle did have a personal vision of France, rooted in the highly literary, religious and nationalistic military culture of the late 19th century. France, he told Malraux, *has been the soul of Christianity . . . of European civilization.*[90] During the RPF period he made a speech celebrating what he called the *three flames* of France: the *social flame; the flame of those who reject social injustice, the specifically Christian flame which comes from the same source as the first . . . finally there is the flame of tradition . . . We cannot build France by constantly denying her past.*[91] De Gaulle's social Catholic heritage was important. He frequently deplored what he saw as the soullessness of modern industrial capitalism, and seemed to believe that Europe, with its classical and medieval Christian heritage, offered a sort of moral third way between unfettered *laissez-faire* liberalism (the 'Anglo-Saxon' model) and despotic socialism (the Russian model). (It is unclear whether he thought these values were essentially French or European but in a sense the question was redundant: for de Gaulle Europe was a continuation of France by other means.)

Yet in the 1960s de Gaulle presided over a dramatic transformation of France which dealt a death blow to most of the cultural values of his upbringing: the peasant disappeared, society became more secular and the hypermarket, rock music, jeans, high-rise flats, television and mass consumerism all arrived on the scene. Much of this was strange and probably antipathetic to him, but he accepted and embraced its necessity. For de Gaulle, the interests of France could not be served by a sentimental nostalgia, even if for people of his generation and background this involved, as he put it, a *victory over oneself*, over inherited attitudes and beliefs. To quote one celebrated television broadcast: *it is quite natural to feel nostalgia for what the empire was, just as one can regret the gentleness of oil lamps, the splendour of sailing ships . . . But no policy that fails to take account of realities is worthwhile* (14 June 1960). He proclaimed that *France has married her century*. At all costs France had to adapt to the modern world: *Once upon a time there was an old country, encased in tradition and caution . . . Now this country has recovered itself . . . We must transform our old country of France into a new country, and it must marry its epoch . . . We must become a great industrial state or resign ourselves to decline* (14 June 1960). Thus modernization was turned into a sort of fairy tale, an epic adventure. As de Gaulle had said in his memoirs about 1940: *Harsh though the realities might be, perhaps I would be able to master them, since it was possible for me, in Chateaubriand's phrase, 'to lead the French by dreams'*. In the 1960s economic change was a reality and a necessity; de Gaulle would turn it into a dream.

This tension between dreams and reality was at the heart of de Gaulle's political action – a balancing of reason and sentiment, of a sense of proportion and visionary ambition (as he often remarked *I have always acted as if . . . and often it did come about*).[92] De Gaulle's words on Moulin could well apply equally well to him: *he was a man of faith and calculation*. De Gaulle encased his passion in ice, his romanticism in classical prose. He celebrated charismatic leadership and pragmatic respect for circumstances: he was a 19th-century romantic nationalist who invoked *Realpolitik*; he disguised the ruthless statecraft of a Cardinal Richelieu in the florid language of a Chateaubriand; he was a rebel who aspired to order, oscillating between action and withdrawal, between exaltation and melancholy.

After his final retirement he started to write what he called his

Jacques Chirac and other Gaullists commemorating de Gaulle's death at the cemetary of Colombey

Memoirs of Hope, but what we know of de Gaulle's private conversation in the last months of his life reveals a mood of brooding pessimism reminiscent of the 1950s: France had fallen back into mediocrity. By this stage in his life de Gaulle had more or less come to identify *grandeur* with himself: by definition, to reject de Gaulle was to choose mediocrity. *They will put up a huge Cross of Lorraine on a hill higher than all the others. Everyone will be able to see it. But as there won't be anyone there, no one will see it. It will incite the rabbits to resistance.*[93] De Gaulle often resorted to this semi-apocalyptic and bleak tone, and it seems to reveal, at the core of the man, a streak of nihilism. *Rien ne vaut rien (nothing is worth anything)*: this phrase of Nietzsche recurs frequently in his conversation. Often also he would repeat a remark that Stalin had made to him: *in the end it is only death that wins.* De Gaulle's consolation for the transience of earthly existence was the permanence of France. The *Memoirs of Hope* begin: *France comes from the depths of the past.* He told Malraux at Colombey that *France lasts longer than the oldest branch in this park.*

De Gaulle was right about the erection of a huge Cross of Lorraine, but he was wrong about the rabbits – and he probably knew it. After his defeat in the referendum of 1969 de Gaulle had told an aide: *the French no longer want de Gaulle. But the myth, you will see the growth of the myth . . . in thirty years*[94] Thirty years later this prediction seems to have been amply fulfilled. In his lifetime de Gaulle excited both fervent adulation and passionate opposition. Indeed no 20th-century French political figure has aroused greater hatred. But as the new century begins, apart from a hard core of nostalgic Pétainists or *pieds noirs* families, de Gaulle seems to inspire almost universal admiration. In the pantheon of French collective memory he is almost on a level with Joan of Arc, Louis XIV and Napoleon. Particularly ironic is the fervent adulation he excites today among leading members of the generation of 1968, who in effect drove him from office. One of them, Serge July, editor of the left-wing newspaper, *Libération,* wrote in 1990: 'nowadays one no longer discusses de Gaulle, one contemplates his legend like a lost continent, that is when one isn't dreaming of it.'[95] In the same year, Régis Debray, who spent 1968 in a Bolivian prison after fighting alongside Che Guevara, wrote: 'de Gaulle fills me with happiness. How comforting it is to imagine that he was alive and in our midst. His name will serve for a long time as an eraser of mediocrity.' He concluded that de Gaulle was the first great man of the 21st century.[96] Of all de Gaulle's many achievements, none will prove more durable than the myth.

Notes

The abbreviation LNC, used in these notes, stands for de Gaulle's *Lettres, notes et carnets* (Paris: 1980–1988). The dates which follow refer to the volume in question.

All the quotations from de Gaulle not referenced in these endnotes come either from his *Memoirs* or from the five collected volumes of his speeches, *Discours et messages 1940–1969* (Paris: 1970–71).

1   J–R Tournoux, *Pétain et de Gaulle* (Paris: 1964), p 88.

2   LNC 1905–18, p 50.

3   LNC 1905–18, p 525.

4   C de Gaulle, *Le Fil de l'épee* (Paris: 1932), p 15.

5   LNC 1919–40, p 457.

6   LNC 1919–40, pp 473–4.

7   D Dilks (ed), *The Diaries of Sir Alexander Cadogan* (London: 1973), p 302.

8   E L Spears, *Fulfilment of a Mission* (London: 1977), p 121.

9   J Harvey (ed), *War Diaries of Oliver Harvey, 1941–45* (London: 1978), pp 163, 224–7.

10   E L Spears, *Two Men who saved France* (London: 1966), p 146.

11   Quoted in J-L Crémieux-Brilhac, *La France Libre: de l'appel du 18 juin à la Libération* (Paris: 1996), p 161.

12   M Borden, *Journey Down a Dark Alley* (London: 1946) pp 113–15.

13   Pierre Brossolette quoted by F Kersaudy, *Churchill and de Gaulle* (London: 1990), p 186.

14   LNC June 1940–July 1941, pp 330–1, 346, 350–2.

15   LNC June 1940–July 1941, p 385. See also H Alphand, *L'Étonnement de l'être* (Paris: 1972), p 11.

16   *The Diaries of Cadogan*, p 635.

17   E Roussel, *Charles de Gaulle* (Paris: 2002), p 432.

18   P Villon, *Résistant de la première heure* (Paris: 1983), pp 117–18.

19   Mauriac, *Un Autre de Gaulle*, p 51.

20   Mauriac, *Un Autre de Gaulle*, p 23.

21   J Charlot, *Le Gaullisme d'opposition* (Paris: 1983), pp 258–9.

22   C Guy, *En Écoutant de Gaulle (Journal 1946–1949)*
     (Paris: 1996) 12 March 1948.

23   J Lacouture, *De Gaulle II: Le Politique* (Paris: 1985), p 313.

24   A Peyrefitte, *C'était de Gaulle* (Paris: 2002), p 291.

25   All these quotations from J-R Tournoux, *La Tragédie du Général*
     (Paris: 1967).

26   D Schoenbrun, *The Three Lives of Charles de Gaulle*
     (London: 1966), pp 94–5.

27   Quoted in A Hartley, *Gaullism* (London: 1972), p 19.

28   J Moch, *Rencontres avec Charles de Gaulle* (Paris: 1971),
     pp 122–23.

29   Guy, *En Écoutant*, p 55.

30   Guy, *En Écoutant*, p 63.

31   De Gaulle, *Le Fil*, p 6.

32   J-R Tournoux, *Jamais dit* (Paris: 1971), pp 70–1.

33   Guy, *En Écoutant*, p 42.

34   LNC 1905–18, pp 336–7.

35   L Joxe, *Victoires sur la nuit: mémoires* (Paris, 1981), p 144.

36   J-R Tournoux, *Pétain et de Gaulle*, p 119.

37   A Malraux, *Les Chênes qu'on abat* (Paris: 1971), pp 73–4.

38   Tournoux, *La Tragédie*, pp 110–11.

39   Malraux, *Les Chênes*, p 166.

40   Peyrefitte, *C'était de Gaulle*, p 394.

41   J Touchard, *Le Gaullisme* (Paris: 1978), p 18.

42   Lacouture, *De Gaulle II*, p 208.

43   J-C Crémieux-Brilhac, 'Introduction' to C de Gaulle,
     Mémoires (Paris: 2000), p xx.

44   O Rudelle, *Mai 1958: de Gaulle et la république*
     (Paris: 1988), p 99.

45 LNC 1951–8, p 235.

46 Tournoux, *La Tragédie*, p 218.

47 Guy, *En Écoutant*, p 207.

48 R Rémond, *Le Retour du général* (Brussels: 1998), p 69.

49 Roussel, *Charles de Gaulle*, pp 598–600.

50 A Dulac, *Nos guerres perdues* (Paris: 1969), pp 88–91; R Salan, *Mémoires III* (Paris: 1972), p 352.

51 For the former view, P-M de la Gorce, *De Gaulle entre deux mondes* (Paris: 1964), pp 569–70; for the latter, Dulac, *Nos guerres*, pp 91, 94; J Soustelle, *Vingt ans de gaullisme* (Paris: 1968), p 147.

52 LNC 1951–8, p 365.

53 Rudelle, *Mai 1958*, p 251.

54 Lacouture, *De Gaulle I*, p 164.

55 Tournoux, *Jamais dit*, p 190.

56 Rudelle, *Mai 1958*, p 59.

57 LNC 1958–1960, p 330.

58 Peyrefitte, *C'était de Gaulle*, p 66.

59 LNC 1958–1960, p 104.

60 LNC 1958–1960, p 331.

61 J Lacouture, *De Gaulle III: Le souverain* (Paris: 1986), pp 102, 136.

62 LNC 1961–63, p 27.

63 Tournoux, *La Tragédie*, p 402.

64 Peyrefitte, *C'était de Gaulle*, p 603.

65 Peyrefitte, *C'était de Gaulle*, pp 296, 807.

66 Peyrefitte, *C'était de Gaulle*, p 306.

67 Peyrefitte, *C'était de Gaulle*, p 616.

68 Peyrefitte, *C'était de Gaulle*, pp 298–9.

69 P Cerny, *The Politics of Grandeur: Ideological Aspects of de Gaulle's Foreign Policy* (Cambridge: 1980), p 131.

70 Tournoux, *La Tragédie*, p 321.

71 Peyrefitte, *C'était de Gaulle*, pp 173, 293, 622.

72 Peyrefitte, *C'était de Gaulle*, p 823.

73 Peyrefitte, *C'était de Gaulle*, pp 323, 329.

74   Peyrefitte, *C'était de Gaulle*, p 300.

75   Cerny, *The Politics of Grandeur*, pp 147, 150.

76   LNC 1961–3, p 94.

77   Peyrefitte, *C'était de Gaulle*, pp 114, 499–500.

78   P Viansson-Ponté, *Histoire de la République gaullienne vol ii* (Paris: 1971), p 184.

79   F Flohic, *Souvenirs d'outre de Gaulle* (Paris: 1979), p 172.

80   Peyrefitte, *C'était de Gaulle*, p 1458.

81   J Foccart, *Journal de l'Elysée. Le Général en mai* (Paris: 1998), p 143.

82   M Droit, *Les Feux du Crépuscule. Journal 1968–1969–1970* (Paris: 1971), p 127.

83   Rudelle, *Mai 1958*, p 293.

84   R Aron, *Mémoires* (Paris: 1983), p 433.

85   Quoted in *Espoir*, June 1983, p 18.

86   Spears, *Two Men*, p 144; Roussel, *Charles de Gaulle*, p 132.

87   C de Gaulle, *La Discorde chez l'ennemi* (Paris: 1924), p 10.

88   C de Gaulle, *La France et son armée* (Paris: 1938), p 51.

89   Malraux, *Les Chênes*, p 37.

90   Malraux, *Les Chênes*, p 145.

91   LNC 1945–51, pp 405–6.

92   Peyrefitte, *C'était de Gaulle*, p 170.

93   Malraux, *Les Chênes*, p 129

94   Quoted in Lacouture, *De Gaulle III*, p 755.

95   *Libération*, 18 June 1990

96   R Debray, *A Demain de Gaulle* (Paris: 1990), p 68.

Chronology

Year	Age	Life
1890		22 November: Charles André Joseph Marie de Gaulle born in Lille.
1895–1900		Educated at primary school of Christian Brothers (Paris).
1900–04		Secondary education at Jesuit College of the Immaculate Conception (Paris).
1905–07		Completes his secondary education at College of the Sacred Heart in Antoing, Belgium, after religious congregations forbidden to teach in France.
1910	19	Enters St Cyr Military Academy.
1912	21	Graduates from St Cyr 13th out of 211, and joins 33rd Infantry Regiment in Arras.
1913	22	Promoted to lieutenant.
1914	23	15 August: wounded at Dinant.
1915	24	February: promoted captain. 10 March: wounded at Mesnil-les-Hurlus (Somme).

1890	In Germany, Otto von Bismarck dismissed. In Spain, universal suffrage.	Tchaikovsky, *The Queen of Spades*. Paul Cézanne, *The Cardplayers*.
1895	In Britain, Lord Salisbury becomes prime minister. Cuban rebellion begins. Japan conquers Formosa (Taiwan). Lumière brothers invent the cinematograph. Guglielmo Marconi invents wireless telegraphy. Wilhelm Röntgen invents X-rays.	H G Wells, *The Time Machine*. W B Yeats, *Poems*. Oscar Wilde, *The Importance of Being Earnest*.
1900	First Pan-African Conference. In France, Dreyfus pardoned. Relief of Mafeking. In China, Boxer Rebellion (until 1901). First Zeppelin flight.	Hector Berlioz, *The Taking of Troy*. Edward Elgar, *Enigma Variations*. Freud, *The Interpretation of Dreams*
1905	Russian revolution against monarchy fails. Bloody Sunday massacre in St Petersburg. Korea becomes protectorate of Japan.	Richard Strauss, *Salome*. Albert Einstein, *Special Theory of Relativity*. Paul Cézanne, *Les Grandes Baigneuses*.
1910	George V becomes king of Britain. Union of South Africa created. Japan annexes Korea.	Constantin Brancusi, *La Muse endormie*. Igor Stravinsky, *The Firebird*. E M Forster, *Howards End*.
1912	Balkan Wars (until 1913). ANC formed in South Africa. *Titanic* sinks. Morocco becomes French protectorate. Dr Sun Yat-sen establishes Republic of China. Stainless steel invented.	Arnold Schoenberg, *Pierrot lunaire*. Carl Jung, *The Psychology of the Unconscious*. Bertrand Russell, *The Problems of Philosophy*.
1913	In US, Woodrow Wilson becomes president (until 1921). In Greece, George I assassinated. In China, rebellion in Yangzi Valley and Yuan Shikai elected president. Hans Geiger invents Geiger counter.	Stravinsky, *The Rite of Spring*. Guillaume Apollinaire, *Les peintres cubistes*. Marcel Proust, *A la recherche du temps perdu* (until 1927).
1914	28 June: Archduke Franz Ferdinand assassinated in Sarajevo. First World War begins. Panama Canal opens. Egypt becomes British protectorate.	James Joyce, *The Dubliners*, Ezra Pound, *Des Imagistes*.
1915	Dardanelles/Gallipoli campaign (until 1916). Italy denounces its Triple Alliance with Germany and Austria Hungary.	John Buchan, *The Thirty-Nine Steps*. D H Lawrence, *The Rainbow*. Ezra Pound, *Cathay*.

Year	Age	Life
1916	25	2 March: wounded and taken prisoner at Dinant.
1918	28	3 December: Returns to France after 32 months in various German Prisoner of War camps.
1919	28	April: attached to Polish army in Warsaw.
1921	30	Returns to France. 7 April: Marries Yvonne Vendroux in Calais.
1922–4		Attends the Ecole Supérieure de la Guerre.
1924	32	Publishes *La Discorde chez l'ennemi*.
1925	33	Attached to staff of Marshal Pétain.
1927	36	April: under patronage of Pétain gives three lectures on leadership to Ecole Supérieure de la Guerre. September: takes command of 19th Battalion of Chasseurs at Trèves.
1929	38	Attached to French army in Lebanon and Syria.
1931	41	November: Returns to France and appointed to the Sécrétariat General de la Défense Nationale.
1932	41	May: death of father, Henri de Gaulle. July: publishes *Le Fil de l'épée (The Edge of the Sword)*.
1933	43	December: promoted to lieutenant colonel.
1934	43	May: Publishes *Vers une armée de metier (Towards an Army of the Future)*.
1935	44	15 March: in parliament, Paul Reynaud advocates ideas on military reorganization inspired by de Gaulle.
1936	45	14 October: has interview with Léon Blum to propose his ideas for military reorganization.

Year	History	Culture
1916	Battle of the Somme. Battle of Jutland. Easter Rising in Ireland. Arabs revolt against Ottoman Turks.	Guillaume Apollinaire, *Le poète assassiné*. G B Shaw, *Pygmalion*. Dada movement launched in Zurich.
1918	Treaty of Brest-Litovsk between Russia and the Central Powers. In Russia, Tsar Nicholas II and family executed. 11 November: Armistice agreement ends First World War. Treaty of Versailles.	Oswald Spengler, *The Decline of the West*, Volume 1. Amédée Ozenfant and Le Corbusier, *Après le Cubisme*. Paul Klee, *Gartenplan. Tarzan of the Apes* with Elmo Lincoln.
1921	National Economic Policy in Soviet Union. Chinese Communist Party founded.	Luigi Pirandello, *Six Characters in Search of an Author*. Chaplin, *The Kid*.
1922	Soviet Union formed. Benito Mussolini's fascists march on Rome.	T S Eliot, *The Waste Land*. Joyce, *Ulysses*.
1924	Vladimir Lenin dies.	Forster, *A Passage to India*. Kafka, *The Hunger Artist*.
1925	Pact of Locarno. Chiang Kai-shek launches campaign to unify China.	Erik Satie dies. F Scott Fitzgerald, *The Great Gatsby*. Kafka, *The Trial*.
1927	Joseph Stalin comes to power. Charles Lindbergh flies across Atlantic.	Martin Heidegger, *Being and Time*. Virginia Woolf, *To the Lighthouse*. BBC public radio launched.
1929	Lateran Treaty. Yugoslavia under kings of Serbia. Wall Street crash. Young Plan for Germany.	William Faulkner, *The Sound and the Fury*. Robert Graves, *Goodbye to All That*. Jean Cocteau, *Les Enfants Terribles*.
1931	King Alfonso XIII flees; Spanish republic formed. Ramsay MacDonald leads national coalition government in Britain. Japan occupies Manchuria.	Rakhmaninov's music banned in Soviet Union as 'decadent'. Antoine de Saint-Exupéry, *Vol de nuit*. Fritz Lang, *M*.
1932	Kingdom of Saudi Arabia independent. Kingdom of Iraq independent. James Chadwick discovers neutron.	Aldous Huxley, *Brave New World*. Jules Romains, *Les hommes de bonne volonté*. Bertolt Brecht, *The Mother*. André Malraux, *La condition humaine*. Gertrude Stein, *The Autobiography of Alice B Toklas*.
1933	Nazi Party wins German elections. Adolf Hitler appointed chancellor. Hitler forms Third Reich. F D Roosevelt president in US; launches New Deal.	
1934	In Germany, the Night of the Long Knives. In China, the Long March (until 1935).	Dmitri Shostakovich, *The Lady Macbeth of Mtsensk*.
1935	In Germany, Nuremberg Laws enacted. Philippines becomes self-governing. Italy invades Ethiopia.	George Gershwin, *Porgy and Bess*. Richard Strauss, *Die Schweigsam Frau*. Marx Brothers, *A Night at the Opera*.
1936	Germany occupies Rhineland. Edward VIII abdicates throne in Britain; George VI becomes king. Léon Blum forms 'Popular Front' government in France. Anti-Comintern Pact between Japan and Germany. Spanish Civil War (until 1939).	Prokofiev, *Peter and the Wolf*. A J Ayer, *Language, Truth and Logic*. BBC public television founded.

Year	Age	Life
1937	46	July: takes command of 507th Tank Regiment at Metz.
	47	December: promoted to colonel.
1938	47	September: publishes *La France et son armée France and her Army*.
1939	48	Given command of the tank units of the Fifth Army.
1940	49	21 January: addresses a memorandum on the use of tanks to 80 leading political and military figures. 21 March: Paul Reynaud becomes premier. 15 May: given command of Fourth Armoured Division (4th DCR). 17 May: counter-offensive of 4th DCR at Montcornet. 19–20 May: counter-offensive of 4th DCR at Laon. 25 May: promoted to Brigadier-General. 27–30 May: counter-offensive of 4th DCR at Abbeville. 5 June: appointed Under-Secretary of State for War in Reynaud government. 17 June: leaves France for London. 18 June: makes speech on the BBC calling for continued resistance. 16 July: death of mother, Jeanne, at Paimpont. 3 August: sentenced to death in absentia by a military tribunal at Clermont Ferrand. 7 August: signature of official agreement between British government and the Free French. 26–29 August: territories of French Equatorial Africa rally to de Gaulle. 25 September: Franco-British expedition to Dakar is repelled. 8 October: visits Doula in Cameroon
1941	49	March–September: in Middle East. 24 September: sets up French National Committee. October: Jean Moulin arrives in London.
	50	December: Free French take over St. Pierre et Miquelon.
1942	50	8 April: Laval returns to power at Vichy. April: drafts a 'Declaration' to the Resistance. 11 June: victory of Free French troops at Battle of Bir Hakeim.
1943	52	January: meets Roosevelt at Anfa (Casablanca) conference. 31 May: arrives in Algiers. 3 June: CFLN set up. 9 November: Giraud removed from CFLN.

1937	Arab-Jewish conflict in Palestine. Japan invades China. Nanjing massacre.	Jean-Paul Sartre, *La Nausée*. John Steinbeck, *Of Mice and Men*. Picasso, *Guernica*.
1938	Kristallnacht: in Germany, Jewish houses, synagogues and schools are burnt down, and shops looted. Austrian Anschluss with Germany. Munich Crisis. Czechoslovakia cedes Sudetenland.	Elizabeth Bowen, *The Death of the Heart*. Graham Greene, *Brighton Rock*. Evelyn Waugh, *Scoop*. Eisenstein, *Alexander Nevsky*.
1939	Stalin and Hitler sign non-aggression pact. 1 September: Germany invades Poland. Russo-Finnish War begins. Francisco Franco becomes dictator of Spain. Britain and France declare war on Germany.	Steinbeck, *The Grapes of Wrath*. John Ford, *Stagecoach* with John Wayne. David O Selznick, *Gone with the Wind* with Vivien Leigh and Clark Gable.
1940	Germany occupies France, Belgium, the Netherlands, Norway and Denmark. In France, Vichy government established. Britain retreat from Dunkirk. Winston Churchill becomes PM. Battle of Britain begins. Leon Trotsky assassinated in Mexico.	Graham Greene, *The Power and the Glory*. Ernest Hemingway, *For Whom the Bell Tolls*. Chaplin, *The Great Dictator*. Disney, *Fantasia*.
1941	Operation Barbarossa: Germany invades Soviet Union. Churchill and F D Roosevelt sign Atlantic Charter. Japan attacks Pearl Harbor. US enters Second World War. In US, Manhattan Project begins.	Bertolt Brecht, *Mother Courage and her Children*. Orson Welles, *Citizen Kane*.
1942	Battle of Stalingrad. Battle of Midway. Battle of El Alamein. First V2 rocket launch. Enrico Fermi conducts controlled chain-reaction in first nuclear reactor.	Dmitri Shostakovich, Symphony No. 7. Frank Sinatra makes stage debut in New York. Albert Camus, *L'Etranger*. Jean Anouilh, *Antigone*.
1943	Allies bomb Germany. Battle of Kursk. Allies invade Italy: Mussolini deposed. Tehran Conference. Lebanon becomes independent. Albert Hoffman discovers hallucinogenic properties of LSD.	Richard Rodgers and Oscar Hammerstein, *Oklahoma*. Jean-Paul Sartre, *Being and Nothingness*. T S Eliot, *Four Quartets*.

Year	Age	Life
1944	53	20 March: Pucheu executed in Algiers. 3 June: declares CFLN the Provisional Republic. 14 June: visits Bayeux. 25 August: arrives in Paris. 26 August: procession down Champs Elysées. 14–18 September: visits Lyons, Marseilles, Toulouse, Bordeaux. 24 October: de Gaulle's Provisional Government recognized by Britain, Soviet Union and the US.
	54	24 November–16 December: visits Moscow.
1945	54	13 February: refuses Roosevelt's invitation to meet him after Yalta. 7 August: commutes death penalty on Marshal Pétain to life imprisonment. 13 November: elected head of provisional government by Constituent Assembly.
1946	55	20 January: resigns from power. 16 June: makes speech at Bayeux on reform of the state.
1947	56	7 April: announces creation of RPF. 19 and 26 October: RPF wins 40 per cent of vote at municipal elections.
1947-52	56	Visits every Department in France to support RPF.
1951	60	June: RPF wins only 22 per cent at legislative elections.
1952	62	27 December: cataract operation.
1953	62	6 May: announces that RPF will play no further role in parliamentary politics.
1954	63	22 October: publication of first volume of *War Memoirs*.
1955	64	13 September: announces the dissolution of the RPF. 8 June: publication of second volume of *War Memoirs*.
1958	67	15 May: announces he is 'ready to assume the powers of the Republic'. 19 May: gives press conference. 27 May: announces he has begun process of forming a government. 1 June: de Gaulle government approved in parliament. 3–7 June: visit to Algeria; announces 'I have understood you.' 14 September: receives Konrad Adenauer at Colombey. 17 September: addresses memorandum on 'Atlantic Directory' to Eisenhower and Macmillan. 28 September: constitution of Fifth Republic approved by referendum. 3 October: announces 'Constantine Plan' for Algeria. 13 October: offers FLN 'peace of the brave'.
	68	21 December: elected President of Fifth Republic.

Year	History	Culture
1944	Normandy invasion. Paris is liberated. Arnhem disaster. Civil war in Greece.	Jorge Luis Borges, *Fictions*. Eisenstein, *Ivan the Terrible*. Laurence Olivier, *Henry V.*
1945	Yalta Agreement. 8 May: Germany surrenders. United Nations formed. Potsdam conference. Harry Truman becomes US president. Atomic bombs dropped on Hiroshima and Nagasaki. UNESCO founded. 2 September: Japan surrenders.	Benjamin Britten, *Peter Grimes*. George Orwell, *Animal Farm*. Karl Popper, *The Open Society and Its Enemies*.
1946	Cold War begins. Italian Republic formed. In Argentina, Juan Perón becomes president. Jordan becomes independent.	Russell, *History of Western Philosophy*. Sartre, *Existentialism and Humanism*. Eugene O'Neill, *The Iceman Cometh*.
1947	Puppet Communist states in eastern Europe. India becomes independent. Chuck Yeager breaks the sound barrier.	Tennessee Williams, *A Streetcar named Desire*. Camus, *The Plague*. Jean Genet, *The Maids*. Brecht, *The Caucasian Chalk Circle*. Greene, *The Heart of the Matter*. Norman Mailer, *The Naked and the Dead*. Alan Paton, *Cry, the Beloved Country*. Vittorio De Sica, *Bicycle Thieves*.
1951	Anzus pact in Pacific. Colombo Plan. In Britain, Churchill becomes PM again.	Igor Stravinsky, *Rake's Progress*. J D Salinger, *Catcher in the Rye*.
1952	European Coal and Steel Community formed; Britain refuses to join.	Hemingway, *The Old Man and the Sea*. Samuel Beckett, *Waiting for Godot*.
1953	Egyptian Republic formed. Mau Mau rebellion in Kenya (until 1957). Dwight Eisenhower inaugurated US president.	William Burroughs, *Junkie*. Dylan Thomas, *Under Milk Wood*. Miller, *The Crucible*.
1954	French surrender at Dien Bien Phu. Rebellion in Algeria.	Britten, *The Turn of the Screw*. William Golding, *Lord of the Flies*.
1955	West Germany joins NATO. Warsaw Pact formed.	Baldwin, *Notes of a Native Son*. Vladimir Nabokov, *Lolita*.
1958	Pope John XXIII elected. Great Leap Forward launched in China (until 1960). Castro leads communist revolution in Cuba. Texas Instruments invents silicon chip.	Chinua Achebe, *Things fall Apart*. Boris Pasternak, *Dr Zhivago*. J K Galbraith, *The Affluent Society*. Claude Lévi-Strauss, *Structural Anthropology*. Harold Pinter, *The Birthday Party*.

Year	Age	Life
1959	68	16 September: announces plan for Algerian self-determination.
1960	69	24 January: 'barricades week' begins in Algiers.
		29 January: television appearance calling on Algerian rebels to submit.
		10 June: receives Si Salah at Elysée.
		14 June: television appearance calling for emancipation of Algeria.
		June/July: abortive negotiations between French and FLN at Melun.
	70	9–12 December: last visit to Algeria.
1961	70	8 January: Algerian self-determination approved by 75 per cent in referendum.
		23 April: denounces putsch on television.
		25 April: end of putsch.
		20 May: negotiations begin with FLN at Evian.
		8 September: OAS assassination attempt on de Gaulle.
1962	71	8 April: independence of Algeria approved in referendum.
		14 April: Michel Debré resigns; Georges Pompidou named prime minister.
		22 August: assassination attempt at Petit-Clamart.
		12 September: announces referendum on reform of constitution.
		28 October: reform of constitution approved by 66 per cent of those voting.
	72	25 November: at legislative elections Gaullist UNR wins 229 out of 465 seats.
1963	72	14 January: announces veto of British entry to EEC.
		22 January: signs agreement with Adenauer.
		21 June: France withdraws her Atlantic fleet from NATO.
1964	73	27 January: recognizes People's Republic of China.
		16–19 March: visits Mexico.
		17 April: prostate operation.
		20 September–16 October: visits ten countries in South America.
1965	74	30 January: attends funeral of Churchill in London.
		30 June: suspends French participation in EEC institutions after failure of negotiations on agriculture.
	75	December: at first round of presidential elections de Gaulle obtains only 44 per cent of the vote; at the second round he beats François Mitterrand with 54 per cent of the vote.

1959 Cuban revolution; Fulgencio Batista flees.
Singapore becomes self-governing.

1960 U2 affair. Sharpeville Massacre in South
Africa. Congo becomes independent. Cyprus
becomes independent. Vietnam War begins
(until 1975). OPEC formed. Nigeria
becomes independent. Oral contraceptives
marketed.

Fellini, *La Dolce Vita*.
Alfred Hitchcock, *Psycho*.

1961 Berlin Wall erected. Bay of Pigs invasion.
Yuri Gagarin is first man in space.

The Rolling Stones are formed.
Rudolf Nureyev defects.
François Truffaut, *Jules et Jim*.

1962 Cuban missile crisis. Second Vatican Council
(until 1965). Jamaica, Trinidad and Tobago,
and Uganda become independent.
Satellite television launched.

Alexander Solzhenitsyn, *One Day in the
Life of Ivan Denisovich*.
Wole Soyinka, *The Man Died*.
Edward Albee, *Who's Afraid of Virginia
Woolf?*
David Lean, *Lawrence of Arabia*.

1963 J F Kennedy assassinated; Lyndon Johnson
becomes president of US. Martin Luther
King leads March on Washington.
French veto Britain's bid to join the EEC.

The Beatles, 'She Loves You' and 'I
want to hold your hand'.
Luchino Visconti, *The Leopard*.

1964 Khrushchev ousted by Leonid Brezhnev.
First race relations act in Britain. Civil
Rights Act in US. PLO formed.
Word processor invented.

Saul Bellow, *Herzog*.
Philip Larkin, *The Whitsun Weddings*.
Stanley Kubrick, *Doctor Strangelove*.

1965 Military coup in Indonesia. Indo-Pakistan
War.

The Beach Boys, 'California Girls'.
Joe Orton, *Loot*.
Pinter, *The Homecoming*.
Neil Simon, *The Odd Couple*.

Year	Age	Life
1966	75	7 March: de Gaulle announces withdrawal from NATO.
		11 May: after agreement on agricultural policy is reached France again participates in EEC.
		20–30 June: visits the Soviet Union.
		1 September: speech in Phnom Penh denouncing American involvement in Vietnam.
1967	76	March: Gaullist Party barely retains its majority at parliamentary elections.
		2 June: announces embargo on arms sales to Israel.
		24 July: proclaims 'Vive le Québec libre' in Montréal.
		6-12: visits Poland.
	77	27 November: describes Jews as an 'elite and domineering people' at a press conference.
1968	77	14 May: de Gaulle visits Romania.
		24 May: announces a referendum on 'participation'.
		28 May: Mitterrand announces his candidature for the presidency.
		29 May: de Gaulle visits Baden-Baden.
		30 May: announces dissolution of parliament; huge Gaullist demonstration in Paris.
		30 June: Gaullists win massive majority at parliamentary elections; Maurice Couve de Murville appointed prime minister.
1969	78	February-2 March: receives President Nixon warmly in Paris.
		11 March: announces referendum on regionalisation and reform of Senate.
		27 April: 53 per cent of population votes 'no' in referendum; de Gaulle resigns.
		10 May–19 June: visits Ireland during presidential elections.
		15 June: Pompidou elected president.
1970	79	4-26 June: visits Spain.
		23 October: publication of first volume of *Memoirs of Hope*.
		9 November: dies at Colombey.
		12 November: memorial service at Notre Dame; funeral at Colombey in the afternoon.

Year	History	Culture
1966	Indira Gandhi becomes prime minister of India. H F Verwoerd, prime minister of South Africa, is assassinated. Botswana becomes independent. In China, Cultural Revolution (until 1968).	Graham Greene, *The Comedians*. Sylvia Plath, *Ariel*. Jean Rhys, *The Wide Sargasso Sea*.
1967	Six Day War. Biafra War (until 1970). First heart transplant.	Beatles, *Sergeant Pepper's Lonely Hearts Club Band*. Harrison Birtwistle, *Punch and Judy*. Gabriel García Márquez, *One Hundred Years of Solitude*. Tom Stoppard, *Rosencrantz and Guildenstern are Dead*.
1968	M L King assassinated. Warsaw Pact invade Czechoslovakia. In Vietnam, Tet offensive.	Kubrick, *2001: A Space Odyssey*. The Rolling Stones, *Beggar's Banquet*. Michel Foucault, *The Archaeology of Knowledge*.
1969	Irish troubles begin. Nixon becomes US president. Sino-Soviet frontier war. In Libya, Gaddafi comes to power. First man on moon.	Kenneth Clark, *Civilization*. Mario Puzo, *The Godfather*. *Easy Rider* with Dennis Hopper and Peter Fonda.
1970	Israel and Syria clash over Golan Heights. Northern Ireland riots; IRA provisionals recruits. In Chile, Allende becomes president.	Simon and Garfunkel, *Bridge Over Troubled Water*. Germaine Greer, *The Female Eunuch*. Ken Loach, *Kes*.

Further Reading

The literature on de Gaulle is immense. In 1990 it was estimated to run to over 3000 items, and it has massively increased since then. The fullest bibliographies can be obtained from the website of the Institut Charles-de-Gaulle www.charles-de-gaulle.org. The Institut, situated at 7 Rue Solférino, 75007 Paris, where de Gaulle had his offices between 1947 and 1958, has a great deal of material relating to de Gaulle's life, and publishes a journal devoted to de Gaulle, *L'Espoir,* which appears three times a year.

The best place to begin, however, is with de Gaulle's own writings. The following are available in English: the three volumes of *War Memoirs* – *Call to Honour: 1940–1942* (London: 1955), *Unity: 1942–1944* (London: 1959) and *Salvation: 1944–1946* (London: 1960) – and the unfinished *Memoirs of Hope: Renewal 1958–1962* and *Endeavour 1962–* (both London: 1971). The four books de Gaulle wrote before 1940, all now exist in translation: *The Enemy's House Divided* (Duke, N.C. 2002) *The Edge of the Sword* (London: 1960), *The Army of the Future* (London: 1940) and *France and her Army* (London: 1945). In French only are the five volumes of speeches, *Discours et messages 1940–1969* (Paris: 1970–71), and the thirteen volumes of letters and notes, *Lettres, notes et carnets* (Paris: 1980–97). All these writings have been published under the supervision of de Gaulle's family, and there is much material that has been withheld from publication. They cannot be said to constitute a proper scholarly edition. On the other hand, there is now a proper critical edition of de Gaulle's memoirs in French published in the celebrated Pléiade edition: *Mémoires* (Paris: 2000).

A huge international conference was held in Paris on the 20th anniversary of de Gaulle's death. Its proceedings, published in seven volumes, Institut Charles-de-Gaulle, *De Gaulle en son siècle* (Paris: 1991–3) contain a huge amount of information, but the quality of the contributions varies enormously. There are two superb French biographies. The more recent of these, E Roussel, *Charles de Gaulle* (Paris: 2002) is only available in French. It is the most thoroughly documented work on de Gaulle. The slightly older three-volume study by J Lacouture, *De Gaulle* (Paris: 1984–6), which runs to over 3000 pages in French, is available in a slightly abbreviated two-volume English translation: *De Gaulle: the Rebel* (London: 1989) and *De Gaulle: the Ruler* (London: 1992). There are many readable English biographies including B Ledwidge, *De Gaulle* (London: 1982), A Shennan, *De Gaulle* (London: 1993), C Williams, *The Last Great Frenchman: a Life of Charles de Gaulle* (London: 1995). H Gough and J Horne, *De Gaulle and Twentieth-century France* (London: 1994) contains essays on most aspects of de Gaulle's career by leading French and British historians. S Servais, *Regards sur de Gaulle* (Paris: 1990) is a useful collection of testimonies from a wide range of de Gaulle's contemporaries.

Many of de Gaulle's aides and advisers recorded his conversation, and this is one of the best ways of getting a flavour of the man and a window onto his view of the world. For the period of the Liberation and after see C Mauriac, *The Other de Gaulle: Diaries, 1944–1954* (London: 1973). For the early RPF years see C Guy, *En Écoutant de Gaulle: Journal (1946–1949)* (Paris: 1996). For the Fifth Republic, A Peyrefitte produced almost 2000 pages of de Gaulle's conversation in three volumes, now usefully collected in one: *C'était de Gaulle* (Paris: 2002). The two volumes of J Foccart, *Journal de l'Elysée vol 1: Tous les soirs avec de Gaulle, 1965–1967* (Paris: 1997) and *Vol 2: Le Géneral en mai, 1968–1969* (Paris: 1998) also have a lot of useful material. F Flohic, *Souvenirs d'outre de Gaulle* (Paris: 1979) covers the period after de Gaulle's final retirement. A Malraux, *Fallen Oaks* (London: 1972) purports to be an account of Malraux's last meeting with de Gaulle in December 1969. Doubtless de Gaulle did not utter all the *mots* that Malraux puts in his mouth here, but the book is nonetheless a bravura exercise and a classic work of Gaullist mythology. A huge amount of de Gaulle's conversation was collected in volumes by the journalist J-R Tournoux: *Pétain et de Gaulle* (Paris: 1964), *La Tragédie du Général* (Paris: 1967), *Jamais dit* (Paris: 1971). Although Tournoux does not usually give the source of much of his information, he was certainly well informed and the books remain extremely useful.

For histories covering specific aspects of de Gaulle's career see J-C Crémieux-Brilhac, *La France libre: De l'appel du 18 juin à la libération* (Paris: 1996) for the Free French period; F Kersaudy, *Churchill and de Gaulle* (London: 1981) for de Gaulle in London; Fondation Charles-de-Gaulle and University of Bordeaux-III, *De Gaulle et le RPF (1947–1955)* (Paris: 1998) and J Charlot, *Le Gaullisme d'opposition* (Paris: 1983) for the RPF years; R Rémond, *Le Retour du général* (Brussels: 1998) and O Rudelle, *Mai 1958: de Gaulle et la république* (Paris: 1988) for de Gaulle's return to power in 1958 and the foundation of the new Republic; M Vaïsse, *La Grandeur. Politique étrangere du général de Gaulle (1958–1969)* (Paris: 1998) for de Gaulle's foreign policy in the Fifth Republic. P Cerny, *The Politics of Grandeur: Ideological Aspects of de Gaulle's Foreign Policy* (Cambridge: 1980) is very obviously the work of a political scientist, but remains worth reading. On the Gaullist party in the Fifth Republic, see J Charlot, *The Gaullist Phenomenon: the Gaullist Movement in the Fifth Republic* (London: 1971).

For de Gaulle's political ideas see A Hartley, *Gaullism: The Rise and Fall of a Political Movement* (London: 1972) and J Touchard, *Le Gaullisme (1940–1969)* (Paris: 1978). D Johnson, 'The Political Principles of General de Gaulle' in *International Affairs* (1965) offers a useful introduction. There are also brilliant essays on the subject by S Hoffmann in his *France: Decline and Renewal* (New York: 1974).

For Gaullism after de Gaulle, the standard work is now A Knapp, *Gaullism since de Gaulle* (London: 1993). Also worth reading is M Agulhon, *De Gaulle: Histoire, symbole, mythe* (Paris: 2000), a superb essay on the myth of de Gaulle in France today.

Picture Sources

Archives de Gaulle: p 56; Ann Ronan: pp 11, 15, 26, 28, 29, 33, 38, 39, 45, 47, 51, 77, 83, 85, 90, 93, 115, 125; Gamma: pp 121, 142; Giraudon/Bridgeman Art Library: pp 2, 3, 4; Topham: pp iii, 6, 12, 14, 17, 23, 87, 95, 106, 122, 130; ARJ: p 92; Coll-DITE USIS: p 32; Hachedé: pp 74, 75; Keystone: pp 21, 126; Oasis: p 34; Roger Viollet: p 101

Index

Cambodia, 103, 104
Canada, 105, 106, 129
Capet, Hugues, 61
Cartier, Jacques, 106
Casablanca, 20
Cassin, René, 15, 16, 23
Catalaunian Fields, Battle of the, 69
Catholic Church, 2, 65; schools, 3
Catroux, General Georges, 15–16, 25
Challe, General, 79, 88
Charlemagne, 101
Chateaubriand, Vicomte de, 57, 67, 130, 141
China, 39, 103, 108, 130
Chirac, Jacques, 136, 142
Churchill, Winston, 13–14, 16–20, 25, 27, 37, 50; on Europe, 38, 100; colonial politics, 40–41; as leader, 54; on de Gaulle's capacity for suffering, 58
Claudel, Paul, 57, 130
Clausewitz, Karl Marie von, 67
Clemenceau, Georges, 53, 54, 61
Clovis, 61
cohabitation, 136
Cold War, 34, 45, 49, 97, 108
collaboration, 22, 35
Colombey-les-deux-Églises, 56–7, 68, 71, 74, 76, 124, 126, 142–3; topography, 5, 139; Adenauer visits, 101; de Gaulle buried at, 130
Combat, 36
Communism, 10, 31, 97; de Gaulle's opposition to, 45, 47, 49–50, 81; Soviet, 94, 95, 107
Communists, 8, 31, 33–4, 35, 36, 42, 45–6, 66; 'separatist', 46, 48
Constantine, 83
contraception, legalization of, 123
Corneille, Pierre, 57, 67
Corsica, 74
Coty, René, 76, 77, 136

Couve de Murville, Maurice, 35, 128–9
Cuban missile crisis, 98
d'Argenlieu, Admiral Thierry, 41

Dakar, 14, 18, 19, 70
Dante, 100
Darlan, Admiral Jean François, 20, 21, 22
D-day, 27, 28
de Gaulle, Anne, 56
de Gaulle, Charles: leaves France for London, 1, 12, 139; wartime broadcasts, 1–2, 12–13, 14, 22, 24, 27, 114, 140; family, 2–3; religion, 3, 57; and literature, 4, 52, 57; army career, 4–7, 11; aloofness, 5; marriage, 5; conspicuous height, 5, 6, 56; prisoner of war, 5, 6, 55, 70; sense of destiny, 5, 52–3; indifference to danger, 6; controversial writings, 7; nationalism, 8–10, 93, 139; influence of Péguy, 9, 10; relationship with Pétain, 13; and Churchill, 13–14, 16–20, 25, 27, 37, 38; intransigence, 16–17; psychology, 17–18; forms National Committee, 19; and Roosevelt, 19–22, 24–7, 31, 38–9; commitment to democracy, 22–3, 24, 50, 63–4, 66, 76, 133; political radicalization, 23–4, 31; struggle for power with Giraud, 24–5, 50; forbidden to leave London, 25; leaves London, 25; return to Paris, 29, 31–2, 120; Champs Elysées parade, 32–3, 55, 63–4, 67, 69; truculence, 33; economic policies, 34–6, 64–5, 112, 117, 118, 121, 122, 128, 135; commutes death sentences, 35–6; colonial policies, 41; lack of political base, 42; retirement (1946), 43,

53, 55; RPF period, 44–51, 63, 65, 70, 140; speeches, 45, 60; anti-Communism, 45, 47, 49–50, 81; suspicion of America, 46; retirement (1955), 51, 71; 'de Gaulle' persona, 52–5; physical awkwardness, 55–6; cataract operations, 56; family life, 56–7; conversation, 57; remoteness, 58–60; concept of legitimacy, 62–3, 89, 114, 128, 132; belief in the strong state, 63, 65, 67, 135; hatred of party, 64, 66, 67; social policies, 65; characteristic vocabulary, 67–8; return to power, 70–79; 'the crossing of the desert', 70; pessimism, 70, 127, 142; Algerian war and independence, 71–3, 79–93, 98, 110–12, 114, 133–4; elected President of Fifth Republic, 80; idea of the army, 88–9; assassination attempts, 90, 112; foreign policy, 94–109, 111, 128, 134; visits Germany, 102; hostility to America, 102–3, 112; visits Russia, 103; visits Canada, 105, 106; reconciliation with Britain and America, 107; constitution and style of government, 109–13; rhetorical skills, 114–16, 123; re-elected president, 119–20; events of 1968, 122–9; secret journey to Germany, 126–7; affinity for Ireland, 129; death and funeral, 130–31; ambitions for France, 137–40; dreams and reality, 141; nihilism, 142; *The Edge of the Sword*, 7, 54–5, 58, 88–9, 132, 138; *The Enemy's House Divided*, 7, 88; *France and her Army*, 9, 13, 88, 137; *Towards an Army of the Future*, 7, 88; *Memoirs of Hope*, 82, 130, 142; *War Memoirs*, 5, 31, 34, 52, 60, 63, 70, 94

de Gaulle, Henri, 3
de Gaulle, Mme (Yvonne Vendroux), 5, 56–7
de Gaulle, Philippe, 13
de Gaulle, Xavier, 5
de Lattre de Tassigny, General, 37
de Retz, Cardinal, 42
de Valera, Éamon, 129, 139
Debray, Régis, 143
Debré, Michel, 80, 88, 92, 110–11, 113
Defferre, Gaston, 135
Delebecque, Léon, 72, 73, 76
Delouvrier, Paul, 79
democracy, 22–3, 24, 50, 63–4, 66, 76, 133
Dewavrin, André, 15
Doula, 52
Dreyfus Affair, 2, 10
Dulac, General, 77, 78

Eden, Anthony, 17, 25
Eisenhower, Dwight D, 27, 31, 37–8, 98
Erhard, Ludwig, 102
Europe, 95–102, 108, 140; steel and coal community, 135
European Commission, 94, 102
European Defence Community (EDC), 46, 50
European Economic Community (Common Market), 98–9; British membership, 94, 99–100; agricultural policy, 102
European Union, 136
Evian Accords, 91, 93, 111

Faure, Edgar, 128
FLN (National Liberation Front), 71, 72, 83–4, 86–7, 89–91, 93
Flohic, François, 126
Foccart, Jacques, 104, 124